Private Greeting Cards

P · I · E BOOKS

Private Greeting Cards

P·I·E BOOKS

Villa Phoenix Suite 301, 4-14-6
Komagome, Toshima-ku, Tokyo 170 Japan
Tel: 03-3940-8302 Fax: 03-3576-7361
e-mail: piebooks@bekkoame.or.jp

ISBN4-89444-054-7 C3070

First published in Germany 1998 by:
NIPPAN / Nippon Shuppan Hanbai Deutschland GmbH
Krefelder Straße 85, D-40549 Düsseldorf, Germany
Tel:0211-5048080/89 Fax:0211-5049326

ISBN3-931884-14-7

Printed in Singapore

The designs used on the front cover were provided
by : Bleu Élastique
Katrien Florin & Henk Dezuttere
Sophie Bartho & Associates
Wang & Williams

Contents

Foreword

情報化社会という言葉がすっかり定着してしまった今日ですら、もっと便利な
もの、もっと時間の節約のできるものを追い求める人々の熱意は薄れることが
ない。電話やFAXや電子メールは今や日常生活の必需品の一部となっている。
情報を素早く、お手軽に伝達するにはもってこいのツールだからである。

グリーティング・カードもある意味では情報伝達ツールである。この視点で
とらえると、これ程面倒でまどろっこしいものはない。作成したり、相手に
到達するのに時間がかかる割には、通常の手紙とは違って、その情報量とい
うのは極端に少ない。「メリークリスマス」とか「引っ越しました」「子ども
が生まれました」という事だけを相手に知らせるのに、何故、人はグリーティ
ング・カードを使うのか。FAXや電子メールの方が時間も経費も節減できる
ではないか。そう考える人もいるだろう。しかし、何事もやみくもに便利に
なれば良いというものではない。メッセージの伝達というカードの本質だけ
に囚われてはいけない。そこには、もっと大切な意義が存在するのである。

郵便受けの中に封筒を見つけた時のちょっとした驚きや、封を切り中を取り
出す時のわくわくする気持ち、そしてカードから美しい写真やイラスト、びっ
くりするような仕掛けや楽しいアイデアが飛び出した瞬間の嬉しい気持ち。
カードの送り手は、メッセージと共にこうした気持ちを受け取る側にプレゼ
ントしているのである。

商品のプロモーションDMの様に、「消費者の興味や購買意欲を掻き立てなく
てはならない」という大きな足かせが無い分、個人的なグリーティング・カー
ドのデザインにはふんだんに遊びの要素を盛り込むことができる。この思い
きったデザインというビジュアルな要素が、カードに記された使い古された
言葉を新しく個性的なものに変化させ、受け取る側に新鮮な喜びを与えるの
であろう。

グリーティング・カードは単なるメッセージ伝達ツールではない。郵送とい
う手間のかかる行為と、そのビジュアルイメージによって、言葉だけでは表
現できない気持ちを受け取る側に送ることができる、いわば「粋」なコミュ
ニケーション・ツールなのである。本書に掲載されたグリーティング・カー
ドの受け取り手はあなた自身である。1通1通に込められた想いはあなたに
どのようなメッセージを伝えるのだろうか。

In today's world, and the "information-oriented society" to which we often refer, our passion for convenience and time-saving has never been stronger. Telephones, faxes, and e-mail have already become essential components of our everyday life, simply because they are tools which can deliver information quickly and effortlessly.

In a sense, greeting cards can also be considered tools for information transfer. But considering the amount of time that it takes to create and deliver one, greeting cards differ from normal letters in that the amount of information contained within is very small indeed. Why use a greeting card just to say "Merry Christmas," "I Just Moved," or "We Have A New Baby"? Wouldn't it be faster and easier to send a fax or an e-mail? I'm sure that many people feel that way. However, conveying a message is not the only purpose of a greeting card. There are other important aspects to consider.

The little thrill that one gets when discovering an envelope in the postbox... excitement on opening the envelope and taking out the card... happiness on finding something clever inside... These are some of the "gifts" being sent along with the message.

Private greeting cards can be designed with a sense of fun, as they are not fettered by the need to arouse the consumer's curiosity or motivate them to buy, as are promotional mailings. Their daring visual design elements transform old and overused words into something more personal, bringing the recipient a fresh sense of excitement.

A greeting card is not just a tool for relaying messages. The process of preparing the card, together with the visual images contained within, conveys feelings to the recipient that go beyond the written words. It is really quite a stylish form of communication.

You are the recipient of our greeting card collection. What messages will each of these thoughts bring to you?

In der heutigen Welt und der "Informationsgesellschaft", auf die wir uns oft beziehen, ist unsere Passion für Bequemlichkeit und Zeitersparnis so gross wie nie zuvor. Telefone, Faxe und E-mail sind bereits essentielle Komponenten unseres täglichen Lebens - einfach weil dies Werkzeuge sind, die Informationen schnell und mühelos abliefern.

Auf gewisse Weise kann man auch Grusskarten als Werkzeuge für den Informationstransfer ansehen. Zieht man jedoch den Zeitaufwand in Betracht, eine zu kreieren und letztendlich abzuliefern, so unterscheiden sich Grusskarten von normalen Briefen insofern, als ihr Informationsgehalt wirklich sehr gering ist. Warun eine Grusskarte benutzen, nur um zu sagen "Frohe Weihnachten", "Ich bin umgezogen" oder "Wir haben ein Baby"? Wäre es nicht schneller und einfacher, nur ein Fax zu schicken oder eine E-mail? Ich bin sicher, daß viele Leute so fühlen. Trotzdem ist das Übermitteln einer Botschaft nicht der alleinige Zweck einer Grusskarte. Da sind andere wichtige Aspekte zu bedenken.

Der kleine Schauer, wenn man einen Umschlag im Briefkasten findet... die kleine Aufregung beim Öffnen des Umschlags und beim Herausnehmen der Karte... der Spaß beim Entdecken einer kleinen Überraschung darin... das sind einige der "Geschenke", die zusammen mit der Botschaft ankommen.

Private Grusskarten können mit einem Sinn für Spaß gestaltet werden. Sie sind nicht wie Werbemailings gebunden durch die Notwendigkeit, die Neugier der Kunden zu wecken und sie letztlich zum Kauf zu motivieren. Ihre kühnen visuellen Designelemente transformieren alte und abgenutzte Worte in etwas persönliches und bringen dem Empfänger ein erfrischendes Gefühl der Begeisterung.

Eine Grusskarte ist nicht nur ein Werkzeug, um eine Botschaft zu übermitteln. Der Prozess der Vorbereitung der Karte zusammen mit den visuellen Elementen, die darin enthalten sind, vermitteln dem Empfänger Gefühle, die über das geschriebene Wort hinausgehen. Das ist wirklich eine stilvolle Form der Kommunikation.
Sie sind nun der Empfänger unserer Grusskarten-Kollektion. Welche Botschaft wird jeder dieser Gedanken zu Ihnen bringen?

Editorial Notes

Credit Format クレジットフォーマット

Category of work タイトル
Type of client クライアントの業種
Country from which submitted 国名
Year of completion 制作年
Creative staff 制作スタッフ

CL: *Client*
CD: *Creative director*
AD: *Art director*
D: *Designer*
P: *Photographer*
I: *Illustrator*
CW: *Copywriter*
DF: *Design firm*

タイトルには、作品の使用目的を表記しました。
Categories indicate the purpose of the artwork.

提供者の意向により、クレジットデータの
一部を記載していないものがあります。
Please note that some credit data has been
omitted at the submittor's request.

announcements

SAM GOES TO HOLLYWOOD

marriage announcements birth announcements
change of address notices others

Marriage Announcement
結婚のあいさつ状

Personal／個人
Belgium 1996
CL: Katrien Florin & Henk Dezuttere
CD, AD, D, CW, DF: Katrien Florin /
Henk Dezuttere
P: ABS Tebache

011

Marriage Announcement
結婚のあいさつ状

Personal／個人
Japan 1993
CL, AD, D: 吉田 勝 Masaru Yoshida
CW: 荒川タカユキ Takayuki Arakawa

Wedding Congratulations
ウェディングカード

Greeting Card Company／カード製造販売
USA 1995
CL: Nobleworks
CD, CW: Christopher Noble
AD: Connie Scharar
I: Steven Guarnaccia

P.12 Marriage Announcement
結婚のあいさつ状

Personal／個人
Spain 1994
CL: Santi & Patricia
CD, AD, D: Juan Dávila
D: Laura Meseguer
DF: Cosmic

Marriage Announcement
結婚のあいさつ状

Personal／個人
France 1997
I: François Avril
Illustrator's Agent in Japan: CWC

1,2 Marriage Announcement
結婚のあいさつ状

Personal／個人
Indonesia 1996
CL: Satrija & Lenny (1) / Berry & Yenny (2)
D: Candra Atmaja
I: Li Zi Hua

Marriage Announcement
結婚のあいさつ状

Sculptor & Painter／彫刻家＆画家
Netherlands 1995
CL: Liesbeth Berkers
CD, AD, D, I: Annebeth Nies
DF: Stahl Design

Wedding & New Address Announcement
結婚＆移転通知

Personal／個人
Austria 1995
CL: Silvia & Kurt Dornig
CD, D: Kurt Dornig
P: Reinhard Fasching
DF: Kurt Dornig Grafik-Design & Illustration

OLIVIA RAE LORD • MARCH 23, 1995 • 11:46AM • 7.11LBS • WHITE WITH BROWN TRIM • PERFECT

BABY-O

Birth Announcement
出産通知

Personal／個人
USA 1997
CL: Olivia Rae Lord
CD, AD, D: Peter Lord
D: Elizabeth Carluccio Lord

Birth Announcement
出産通知

Personal／個人
Canada 1990
CL: Zacharko Family
CD, D: Terrance Zacharko
CD, D, CW: Theresa Zacharko
P: Jim LaBounty
DF: Zacharko Design Partnership

Birth & New Address Announcement
出産＆移転通知

Personal／個人
Austria 1996
CL: Anita & Gerd Ludescher
CD, D: Kurt Dornig
DF: Kurt Dornig Grafik-Design & Illustration

1 *Birth Announcement*
出産通知

Personal／個人
Canada 1995
CL: Zacharko Family
CD, D, P: Terrance Zacharko
CD, D, CW: Theresa Zacharko
DF: Zacharko Design Partnership

2 *Birth Announcement*
出産通知

Personal／個人
France 1996
CL: Marie Bortolotti
AD: Pascale Bortolotti
D, I: Frédéric Bortolotti
P: Daniel Pype

WE GOT OUR OWN TURKEY

THIS YEAR
We Celebrated Thanksgiving
THE TRADITIONAL WAY

elle

David Lévy

Mon premier livre

Il leur fit part de son souhait d'avoir

quelqu'un avec qui il pourrait jouer.

1

2

PARENTS: JOHN AND TRUDY ZIELANSKI
BORN: OCTOBER 29, 1994
TIME: 11:30 AM
WEIGHT: 7 LB 13 OZ
LENGTH: 19.25 IN

[SIERRA COLE ZIELANSKI]

SIERRA

3

1 *Birth Announcement*
出産通知

Designer／デザイナー
USA 1995
CL: Denise & Stuart D'Rosario
CD, CW: Stuart D'Rosario
AD: Stefan Sagmeister
D: Veronica Oh
DF: Sagmeister Inc.

2 *Birth Announcement*
出産通知

Personal／個人
Switzerland 1996
CL: Daniel & Leah Lévy
CD, AD, D: Jean-Benoît Lévy
P: Daniel Lévy I: David
CW: Leah Lévy DF: AND Trafic Grafic

3 *Birth Announcement*
出産通知

Personal／個人
USA 1995
CL: The Zielanski Family
AD, D, I, P: Trudy Cole-Zielanski
DF: Trudy Cole-Zielanski Design

1 *Birth Announcement*
出産通知

Personal／個人
Austria 1996
CL: Susi & Robert Brüstle
CD, D, CW: Kurt Dornig
P: Fritz Lampelmayr
DF: Kurt Dornig Grafik-Design & Illustration

2 *Birth Announcement*
出産通知

Personal／個人
Netherlands 1995
CL: Lisa Nuboer & Jeanmarie Dito
CD, AD, D: Ben Faydherbe
P: Jeanmarie Dito
DF: Faydherbe / de Vringer

1

1,2 *Birth Announcement*
出産通知

Personal／個人
France 1995 (2) / 1997 (1)
CL: Mindermann
CD, AD, D, P, I, CW: Pascal Béjean
DF: Bleu Élastique

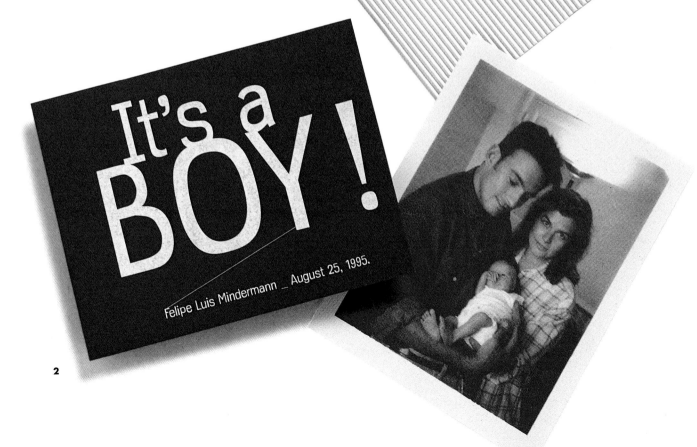

2

Change of Address Notice
移転通知

Personal／個人
Switzerland 1996
CL: Susanne Knecht
AD, D: Lucia Frey / Heinz Wild
DF: Wild & Frey, Agentur für Design

Change of Address Notice
移転通知

Design Firm／デザイン
Switzerland 1996
CL, DF: Wild & Frey, Agentur für Design
AD, D, CW: Heinz Wild

Change of Address Notice
移転通知

Design Firm／デザイン
Korea 1996
CL, DF: Doo Kim Design
CD: Doo Kim
AD: Dongil Lee

Change of Address Notice
移転通知

Design Firm／デザイン
Belgium 1997
CL, DF: Signé Lazer
CD, AD, D, CW: Nathalie Pollet
D, I: Harrisson

1 *Change of Telephone Number Notice*
新電話番号案内

Architects／建築
Netherlands 1992
CL: BNA Architektenburo Roeleveld-Sikkes BV
CD, AD, D: Wout de Vringer
CW: Jan Van Huizen
DF: Faydherbe / de Vringer

2 *Change of Address Notice*
移転通知

Design Firm／デザイン
USA 1995
CL, DF: Sackett Design Associates
CD, AD, D: Mark Sackett
D: Wayne Sakamoto / James Sakamoto

3 *Change of Address Notice*
移転通知

Personal／個人
France 1997
CL: Valérie Justôme & Pascal Béjean
CD, AD, D, P, I, CW: Pascal Béjean
DF: Bleu Élastique

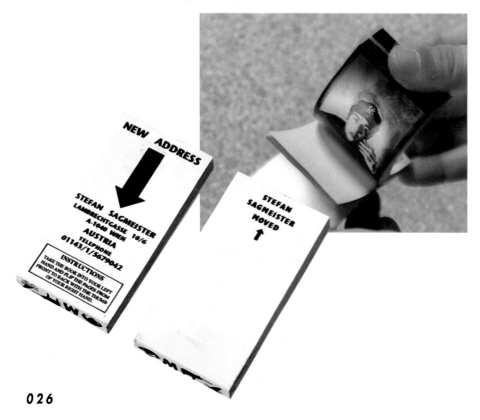

Change of Address Notice
移転通知

Designer／デザイナー
USA 1994
CL: Stefan Sagmeister
CD, AD, D, CW: Stefan Sagmeister
P: Adolf Bereuter
DF: Sagmeister Inc.

パラパラとページをめくると写真が動いて見える。
Flip the pages and the photos will appear to become animated.

Change of Address Notice
移転通知

Design Firm／デザイン
Denmark 1997
CL, DF: Gyllan Grafixx
CD, AD, D: Peter Gyllan

Change of Address Notice
移転通知

Recruiting Firm／就職斡旋業
USA 1995
CL: Janou Pakter, Inc.
CD, AD, D: Marc Hohmann / Akiko Tsuji
P: Christian Witkin @ Nonstøck
DF: Studio Kon/Struktur

Change of Address Notice
移転通知

Design Firm／デザイン
Japan 1997
CL, DF: (有)ヒーター heter inc.
D: 清水正行 Masayuki Shimizu

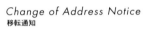

1 *Change of Address Notice*
移転通知

Design Firm／デザイン
USA 1995
CL, DF: White Plus
CD: Trina Nuovo
D: Byron Lee
P: Benson Ng
CW: Daryl Forkell

2 *Change of Address Notice*
移転通知

Art Gallery／ギャラリー
Netherlands 1993
CL: Centrum Beeldende Kunst Dordrecht
CD, AD, D: Wout de Vringer
DF: Faydherbe / de Vringer

3 *Change of Address Notice*
移転通知

Bank／銀行
Austria 1996
CL: Hypo-Bank
CD, D: Kurt Dornig
CW: Hermann Brändle
DF: Kurt Dornig Grafik-Design &
Illustration

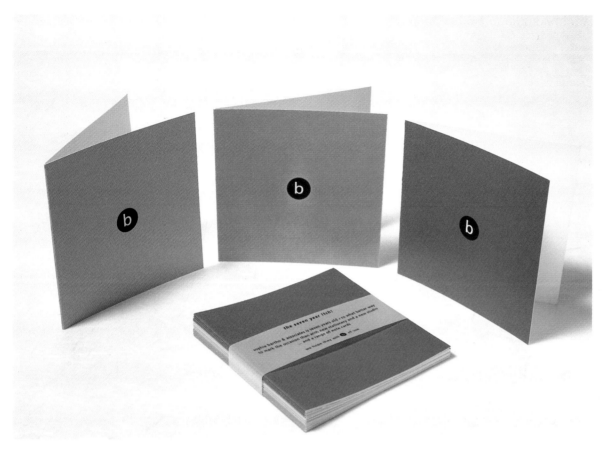

Change of Address Notice
移転通知

Design Consultant／デザインコンサルタント
Australia 1997
CL, DF: Sophie Bartho & Associates
CD, AD, D: Sophie Bartho

Change of Address Notice
移転通知

Design Firm／デザイン
Taiwan 1994
CL, DF: Leslie Chan Design Co., Ltd.
CD, AD, D: Leslie Chan Wing Kei

1 *Change of Area Code Notice*
市外局番変更案内

2 *Change of Address Notice*
移転通知

Design Firm／デザイン
USA 1996
CL ,DF: Mark Oldach Design
CD, AD, D, CW: Mark Oldach

3 *Change of Address Notice*
移転通知

Personal／個人
Japan 1996
CL, CD, AD, D, I, CW: 武曾晋吾 Shingo Muso

4 *Change of Address Notice*
移転通知

Design Firm／デザイン
Japan 1996
CL: ㈲ヨシノデザインオフィス
Yoshino Design Office Inc.
AD, D, CW: 吉野修平 Shuhei Yoshino

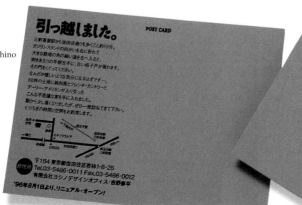

Design Firm／デザイン
Switzerland 1997
CL, DF: Wild & Frey, Agentur für Design
AD, D: Lucia Frey
D: Heinz Wild
P: Pascal Wüest

Change of Address Notice
移転通知

Design Firm／デザイン
Netherlands 1993
CL, I, DF: Studio Boot
CD, AD, D: Petra Janssen / Edwin Vollebergh

Change of Address Notice
移転通知

Illustrator／イラストレーター
Israel 1991
CL, I: Dovrat Ben-Nahum
DF: Studio 106 Tel-Aviv Israel
Illustrator's Agent in Japan: CWC

Change of Address Notice
移転通知

Graphic Designer／グラフィックデザイナー
Netherlands 1994
CL: Martha Lauria
CD, AD, D, CW: Martha Lauria
I: Hendrick Corneliz Vroom
DF: Lauria Grafisch Ontwerp

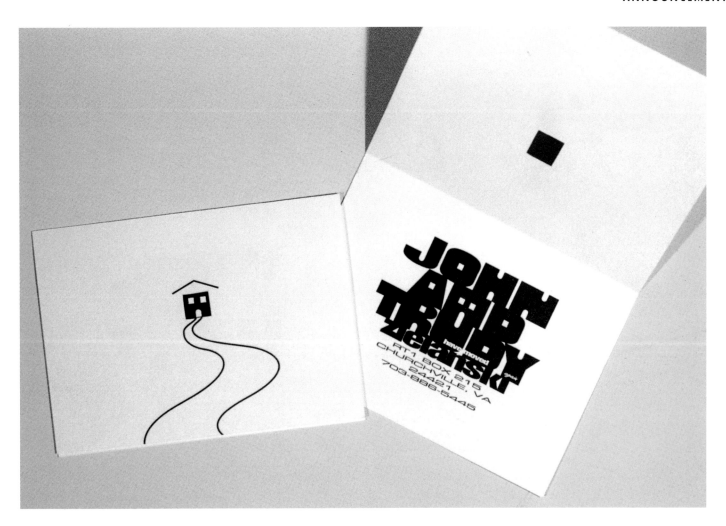

Change of Address Notice
移転通知

Personal／個人
USA 1994
CL: The Zielanski Family
AD, D, I: Trudy Cole-Zielanski
DF: Trudy Cole-Zielanski Design

Change of Address Notice
移転通知

Design Firm／デザイン
USA 1996
CL, DF: Forsythe Design
AD: Kathleen Forsythe
D: Shannon Beer

Change of Address Notice
移転通知

Personal／個人
Netherlands 1993
CL: Arno, Sylvia, David, Yorick & Beau Bauman
D: A. J. Bauman
DF: Studio Bauman BV

Change of Address Notice
移転通知

Design Firm／デザイン
Japan 1996
CL, DF: ㈱アーサー・ハンドレッド・カンパニー
ASA 100 Company
CD, AD, CW: 淺埜 勝 Katsu Asano
D: 米澤帛笑 Kinue Yonezawa

New Office Opening Announcement
事務所開設案内

Design Firm／デザイン
Japan 1997
CL, DF: タカヤグラフィス Takaya Graphis
AD, D: 高西信治 Nobuharu Takanishi

Change of Address Notice
移転通知

Planning & Editorial Office／企画制作・編集
Japan 1997
CL: ㈲プフィス f°ffice Co.
CD, AD, D: 水崎 真奈美 Manami Mizusaki
P: 梅津文彦 Fumihiko Umetsu
CW: 金井ふさ Fusa Kanai

Change of Address Notice
移転通知

Design Firm／デザイン
Japan 1995
CL, DF: ㈱広告丸 Kokokumaru Inc.
AD, D: 高橋善丸 Yoshimaru Takahashi

Competition Announcement
コンペティション案内

Design Firm／デザイン
Netherlands 1996
CL, CD, AD, D: Limage Dangereuse

New Shop Opening Announcement
新店舗オープニング告知

Design Firm／デザイン
Fashion Importer & Retailer／
インポートファッション販売
Japan 1996
CL: ㈱アルトカンポ ALTO CAMPO COMPANY
AD: 高畑 小百合 Sayuri Takahata
D: 高畑三穂 Miho Takahata ／
松井 薫 Kaoru Matsui ／ 久保憲子 Noriko Kubo ／
外崎和子 Kazuko Tonosaki ／
木村智子 Tomoko Kimura ／ 韓 寿江 Sugang Kan

Lecture Announcement
レクチャー案内

Designer／デザイナー
UK 1993
CL: Brian Webb
CD, D: Brian Webb / Lynn Trickett
DF: Trickett & Webb Ltd.

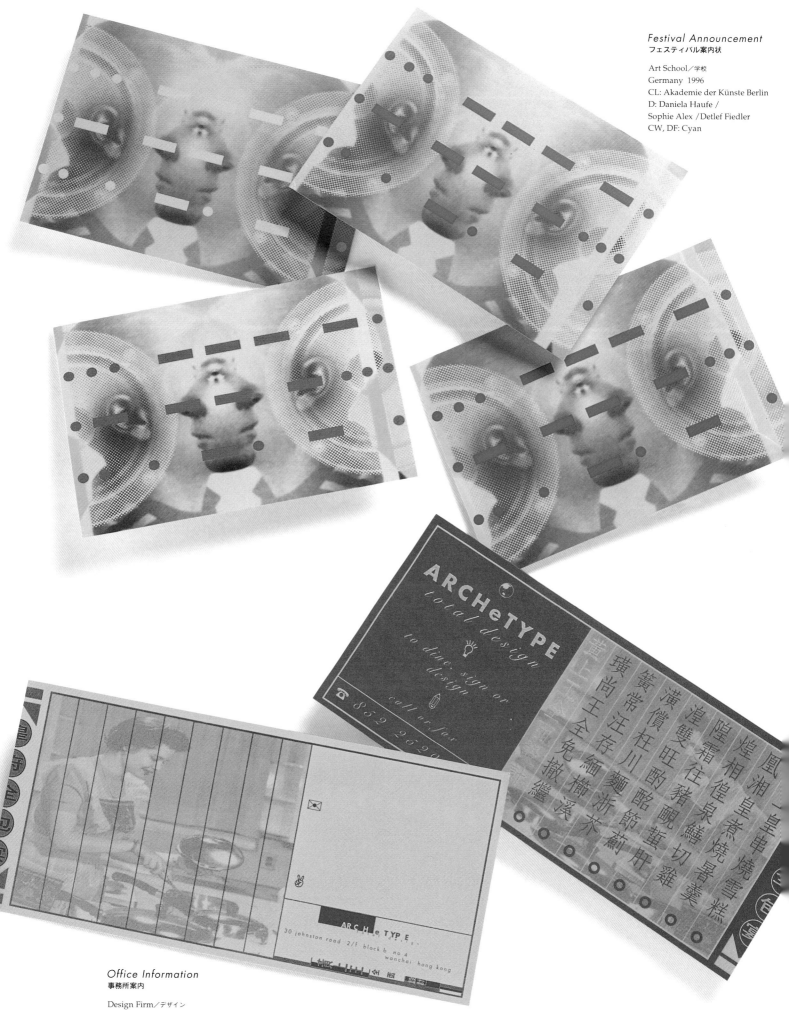

Festival Announcement
フェスティバル案内状

Art School／学校
Germany 1996
CL: Akademie der Künste Berlin
D: Daniela Haufe /
Sophie Alex /Detlef Fiedler
CW, DF: Cyan

Office Information
事務所案内

Design Firm／デザイン
Hong Kong 1995
CL, DF: Archetype Total Design
CD, AD, D: Benjamin Wai Bun Wong
CD: Kacey Kwok Choi Wong

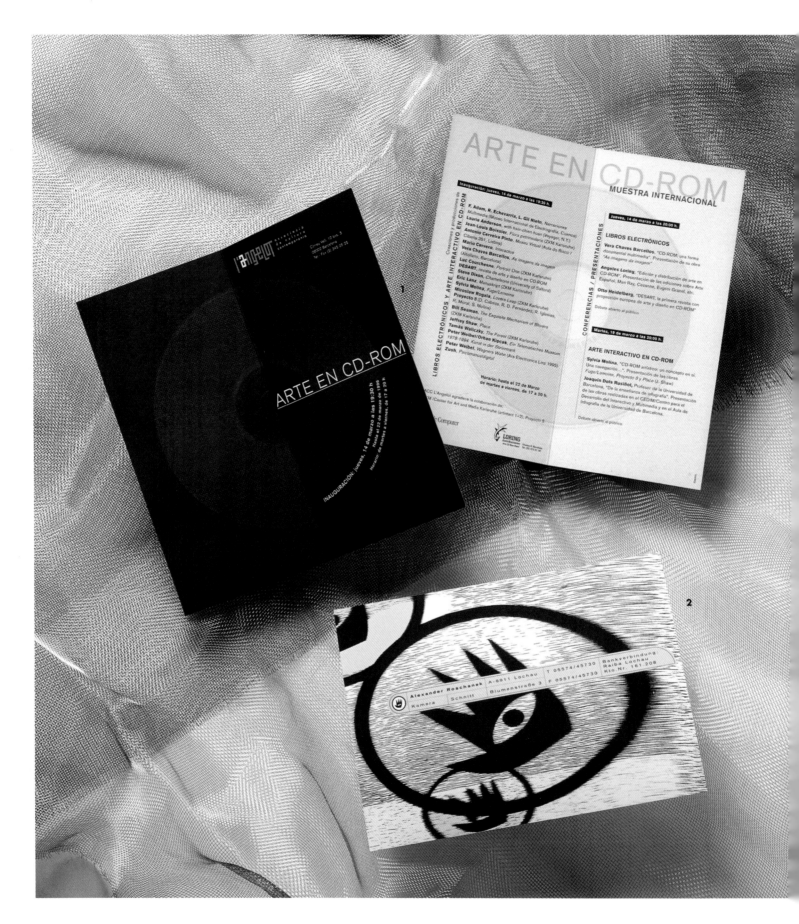

1 *Exhibition Opening Announcement*
展示会オープニング案内

Art Gallery／ギャラリー
Spain 1996
CL: ACC L'Angelot
CD, AD, D: Laura Meseguer
D: Juan Dávila
DF: Cosmic

2 *Company Opening Announcement*
会社設立案内

Cameraman & Editor／写真家＆編集者
Austria 1996
CL: Alexander Roschanek
CD, D: Kurt Dornig
CW: Hermann Brändle
DF: Kurt Dornig Grafik-Design & Illustration

1,2 *Art Auction Announcement*
オークション案内

Art Gallery／ギャラリー
USA 1994 (1) / 1995 (2)
CL: Arts Benicia
AD, D, I: May Liang
DF: May Liang Design

3 *Theatre Schedule*
劇場スケジュール

Theatre／劇場
USA 1997
CL: The Wichita Center for the Arts
CD, AD, D: Sonia Greteman
AD, D, I: James Strange
DF: Greteman Group

1 *Exhibition Announcement*
展示会案内

Academy of Art／教育機関
Netherlands 1996
CL: Academy of Art & Design Denbosch
AD, D: Petra Janssen / Edwin Vollebergh
I, DF: Studio Boot

2 *Festival Announcement*
フェスティバル案内

Movie Festival for Children／映画祭
Netherlands 1993
CL: Cinekid
CD: Jean Philipse / De Studio
AD, D: Petra Janssen / Edwin Vollebergh
I, DF: Studio Boot

3 *New Product & Contest Announcement*
新製品＆コンテスト案内

Children's Clothing Maker &
Electrical Manufacturing Company／
子供服製造販売＆電機メーカー
Netherlands 1996
CL: Oilily / Philips
CD: Jean Philipse
AD, D: Petra Janssen / Edwin Vollebergh
I, DF: Studio Boot

1 *Office Information*
事務所案内

Design Firm／デザイン
Japan 1997
CL, D, DF: ミュゼ Musée
AD: 福田隆志 Takashi Fukuda

2 *Theater Play Announcement*
上演告知

Theatre Company／劇場
Netherlands 1997
CL: Belgisch Toneel Amsterdam
CD: Geert Kimpen
AD, D: Petra Janssen / Edwin Vollebergh
I, DF: Studio Boot

3 *Campaign Announcement*
キャンペーン案内

Charity／チャリティー
Netherlands 1996
CL: Childright Worldwide
AD, D: Petra Janssen / Edwin Vollebergh
I, DF: Studio Boot

手の形をしているステッカーをはがすと下から隠れた
メッセージが出てくる。
Remove the hand-shaped sticker to reveal a hidden message.

New Office Opening Announcement
事務所開設案内

Design Firm／デザイン
Japan 1993
CL: キリマデザイン事務所 Kirima Design Office
AD, D: 切間晴美 Harumi Kirima

New Office Opening Announcement
事務所開設案内

Fortune Teller／占い
Japan 1995
CL: 占星術の館 Holon Nancy Holon
CD, AD, D: 宮本武人 Taketo Miyamoto

New Office Opening Announcement
事務所開設案内

Graphic & Interior Design／
グラフィック＆インテリアデザイン
Germany 1996
CL, DF: AIMO+ Gesellschaft für Gestaltung
CD, CW: Aimo Grebe
AD: Doris Högemann

Wir haben Sommer - behauptet zu-
mindest der Kalender. Und trotz
unserer freundlichen Ankündigung
zur Sommer-Sonnen-Wende müssen
wir feststellen:
Die Sonne versteckt sich verschämt
hinter Wolken, die Temperaturen
scheinen unter Höhenangst zu leiden
und Rasensprenger kennen wir diesen
Sommer nur als Ladenhüter...

Lösen Sie sie ab - und heften Sie sie an.
Und schon haben wir miteinander
etwas bewirkt:
Den gestalterischen Dialog.

Die Wende.
Wir wollen uns abwenden vom be-
liebigen Einerlei hin zum konse-
quenten Stil, abwenden von der
berechnenden Unüberlegtheit zur
besonnenen Vernunft. Abwenden
vom Alltäglichen und Altherge-
brachten zum Ungewöhnlichen
und Neuen.
Aber vor allem wollen wir uns hinwenden:
Hinwenden zu Ihnen und neuen
Perspektiven, hinwenden zur Qua-

1 2 3 4

Opening Announcement
オープニング案内

Marriage Fashion Shop／ウェディングファッション
Austria 1995
CL: Lunardi Marriage Fashion
CD, AD, D: Sigi Ramoser
CD: Sandro Scherling
D: Stefan Gassner
CW: Elke Burtscher
DF: Atelier für Text und Gestaltung

MUSÉE
5 45 8 302
JINGUMAE
SHIBUYA KU
150 TOKYO
034063074
034063627
RYUJI FUKUDA

Office Information
事務所案内

Design Firm／デザイン
Japan 1988
CL, D, DF: ミュゼ Musée
AD: 福田隆志 Takashi Fukuda

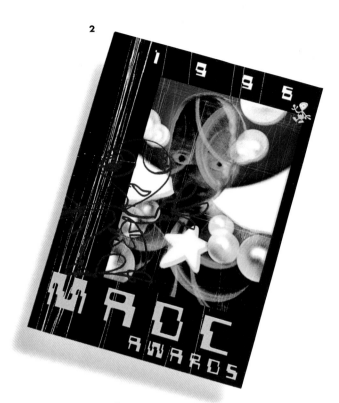

1 *New Office*
Opening Announcement
事務所開設案内

Advertising Agency／広告企画制作
Japan 1995
CL, CD, AD, D, DF: トゥーループ・グラフィックス
TOLOOP graphics

2 *Awards Announcement*
受賞式案内

Design & Advertising Association／
デザイン＆広告協会
Australia 1997
CL: MADC
AD, D: Andrew Hoyne
P: Peter Rosetzky
I: Angela Ho
DF: Andrew Hoyne Design

3 *Notification of Election*
選挙通知

Design Consultancy／
デザインコンサルタント
UK 1997
CL, DF: Design Narrative
CD, AD: Andy Ewan
D: Stephanie Fletcher / Vibe Bangsgaard

4 *New Shop Opening*
Announcement
新店舗オープン案内

Beauty Shop／美容室
Japan 1997
CL: ㈱スティルウォータース Still Waters
AD, D: 駒形克己 Katsumi Komagata
DF: ワンストローク One Stroke Co., Ltd.

invitations

wedding invitations
exhibition invitations   others

Vancouver
4-7
May
95
19
VANCOUVER
VANCOUVER
PICTURE PERFECT
Vancouver

Party Invitation
パーティー招待状

Liquor Distributor／酒類販売
Australia 1996
CL: Swift & Moore
CD: Sophie Bartho
D: Naaz Kerr
DF: Sophie Bartho & Associates

P.46 **Meeting Invitation** 会議招待状

Travel Marketing Company／旅行マーケティング
USA 1995
CL: Cutler Travel Marketing
CD, AD, D, I: John Sayles
CW: Wendy Lyons
DF: Sayles Graphic Design

1 Party Invitation
パーティー招待状

2 Party Invitation
パーティー招待状

Non-profit Organization／非営利団体
USA 1996
CL: Creative Alliance of Pasadena
AD, I: Aram Youssefian
D, I: Benta Kipp
CW: Daryl Forkell
DF: White Plus

Architecture & Design／建築設計, デザイン
USA 1995
CL, DF: NBBJ Graphic Design
D: Daniel R. Smith

1

2

CELEBRATE
10TH ANNUAL BANQUET
THURSDAY, JUNE 13, 1996

10

YOU'RE INVITED
TO HELP US
CELEBRATE 10.

WICHITA INDUSTRIES AND SERVICES FOR THE BLIND

YOU'RE INVITED TO
CELEBRATE
Harvey Hotel
549 S. Rock Road
Wichita, KS 67207
Reception 6:30 P.M.
Dinner 7:00 P.M.
RSVP - by June 4

KEYNOTE SPEAKER
Carl Augusto
Executive Director, American Foundation for the Blind

SPECIAL AWARD PRESENTATIONS
Michael F. Campbell
WISB Pittsburg, National Blind Employee of the Year
Ernest A. Ochel
Member of the NIB Board of Directors

Banquet Invitation
パーティー招待状

Non-profit Organization／非営利団体
USA 1996
CL: Wichita Industries &
Services for the Blind
CD, AD, D: Sonia Greteman
D: Jo Quillin
DF: Greteman Group

The Spice of Life

Spice of Life
Showcase of Services
Tuesday, January 24, 1995

Party Invitation
パーティー招待状

Public Relations／PR
USA 1994
CL: Media Associates
CD, AD, D: Jane Cuthbertson
CW: Media Associates
DF: Myriad Inc.

049

1,2 Golf Competition Invitation
ゴルフコンペ招待状

Film Production／映像プロダクション
Germany 1996 (2) / 1997 (1)
CL: HKF Film-und Fernseh Produktion
AD: Rüdiger Goetz (1)
D, I: Uwe Melichar (1) / Tanja Jacobs (2)
CW: Hannah S. Fricke
DF: Factor Design

Tour Invitation 学校見学招待状

Private School／学校
USA 1992
CL: Dowling High School
CD, AD, D, I: John Sayles
CW: Wendy Lyons
DF: Sayles Graphic Design

Invitation to View New Collection
コレクション招待状

Shoe Company／靴製造販売
Netherlands 1993
CL: Lumberjack
CD: Nico Klerx
AD, D: Petra Janssen / Edwin Vollebergh
I, DF: Studio Boot

Concert Invitation
コンサート招待状

Public Association／公共団体
USA 1996
CL: Des Moines Park & Recreation Department
CD, AD, D, I: John Sayles
DF: Sayles Graphic Design

Speech Invitation
スピーチ招待状

Paper Manufacturer／製紙
USA 1995
CL: James River Corp.
CD, AD, D, I: John Sayles
CW: Wendy Lyons
DF: Sayles Graphic Design

同封された鉛筆をカードの最後のページに差し込むとコマができる。
Push a pencil through the center of the last page of the booklet to make a spinning top.

an ACOUSTIC EVENING with..........

☐ YES! I will attend the Musicians' Assistance Program Benefit at Billboard Live on Friday April 11, 1997.

Enclosed is my check made out to the Musicians' Assistance Program, in the amount of $_____ Contributions are tax deductible only to the extent that they exceed the fair market value (FMV) of the goods and services received.

☐ SORRY, I cannot attend, but would like to make a contribution in the amount of $_____ that will help defray the cost of drug and alcohol treatment. Contributions are fully tax-deductible under I.R.S. section 501 (c) (3).

PLEASE R.S.V.P.
BY MARCH 21, 1997

Fed. I.D. #95.438.3403

Invitation to Benefit チャリティーイベント招待状

Non-profit Organization／非営利団体
USA 1997
CL: Musician's Assistance
AD, D, CW: Ellie Leacock
DF: Art Stuff

ドラッグとアルコールに溺れたミュージシャンを立ち直らせるために活動している団体の主催のファンドレイジング・イベントへの招待状
Invitation to a fund-raising event, sponsored by a group that helps musicians who are recovering from alcohol and drug addictions.

Party Invitation パーティー招待状

Entertainment Production／イベント企画
Mexico 1996
CL: Moctezuma Xocoyotzin
CD, AD, D: Jeronimo Hagerman／
Antonio Sanchez

Birthday Party Invitation
誕生日会招待状

Design Firm／デザイン
USA 1996
CL, DF: Nicosia Creative Expresso Ltd.
CD, AD, D, I: Davide Nicosia

Event Invitation
イベント招待状

Personal／個人
Mexico 1996
CL: Philippe Hernandez
CD, AD, D, I, CW: Antonio Sanchez
DF: El Esqueleto Del Angel (+)

Invitation to Vote 選挙案内

Political Party／政党
Netherlands 1994
CL: D66
AD, D: Petra Janssen / Edwin Vollebergh
I, DF: Studio Boot

Samstag, 25. Jänner 1997 20 Uhr Pfarrsaal Hatlerdorf

Bitte um Antwort bis 15. Jänner 1997

Ich werde vierzig und das möchte ich mit euch feiern.

Birthday Party Invitation
誕生日会招待状

Personal／個人
Austria 1997
CD: Sigi Ramoser
AD: Klaus Österle

COLLEGIUM
INTERNATIONALE
CHIRURGIAE
DIGESTIVAE

XIV Congresso Nazionale
Roma 2 - 4 ottobre 1997

Programma preliminare

Conference Invitation
会議招待状

Medical Association／医療協会
Italy 1997
CL: CICD
AD: Fulvio Caldarelli
D: Mauro Fanti
Project Manager: Monica Solimeno
DF: AREA-Strategic Design

Party Invitation
パーティー招待状

Hairdresser's／美容院
Netherlands 1995
CL: Kapsalon Vollebergh
CD: Gerrit Vollebergh
AD, D: Petra Janssen / Edwin Vollebergh
P: Marie-José Vollebergh / Spierings
I, DF: Studio Boot

055

Reception Invitation
レセプション招待状

Design Firm／デザイン
Netherlands 1996
CL, CD, AD, D: Limage Dangereuse

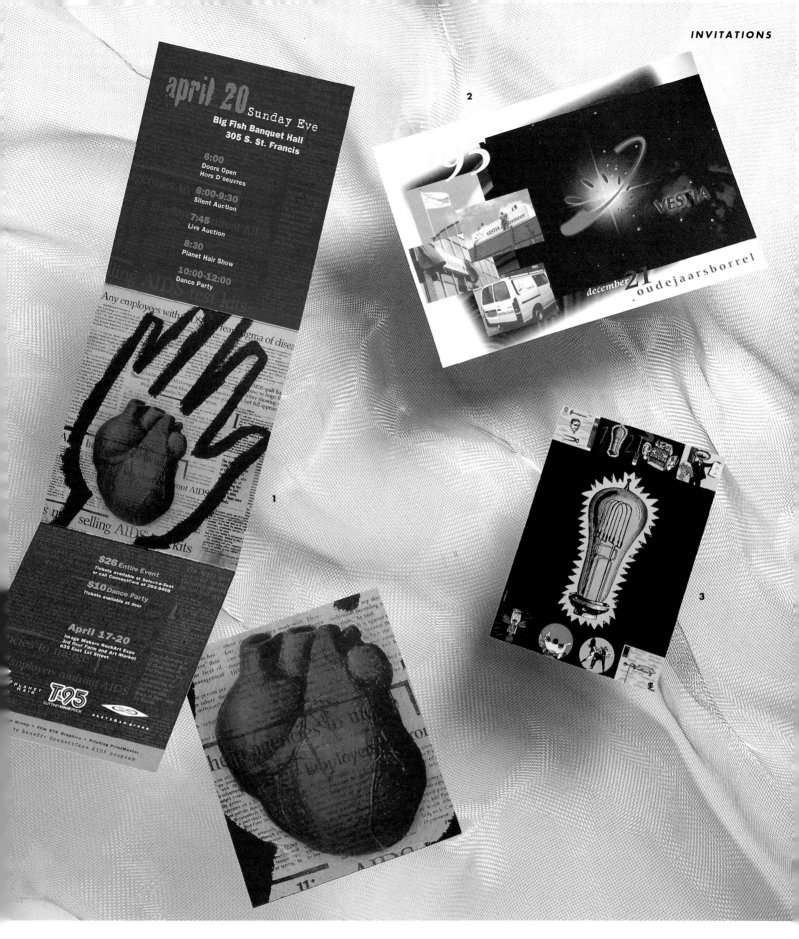

1 *Art Auction Invitation*
オークション招待状

Community Clinical AIDS Program／
民間エイズ医療プログラム
USA 1997
CL: Connect Care
CD, AD, D: Sonia Greteman
AD, D: Jo Quillin
DF: Greteman Group

2 *Party Invitation*
パーティー招待状

Housing Association／住宅供給
Netherlands 1995
CL: Vestia Zoetermeer
AD, D, P, I: Martha Lauria
CW: Vestia Zoetermeer
DF: Lauria Grafisch Ontwerp

3 *CD Presentation Invitation*
CDプレゼンテーション招待状

Music Studio／ミュージックスタジオ
Austria 1997
CL: Anton Studios
CD, D, I: Kurt Dornig
DF: Kurt Dornig Grafik-Design & Illustration

Event Invitation
イベント招待状

International Relations／国際交流
USA 1996
CL: Iowa Council for
International Understanding
CD, AD: John Sayles   D, I: Jennifer Elliott
CW: Kristin Lennert   DF: Sayles Graphic Design

Event Invitation
イベント招待状

Design Foundation／財団
Germany 1996
CL: Bauhaus, Design Foundation
D: Daniela Haufe / Sophie Alex / Detlef Fiedler
CW, DF: Cyan

Invitation to Theatre
劇場招待状

Design Firm／デザイン
Netherlands 1995
CL: Limage Dangereuse
CD, AD, D: Limage Dangereuse
P: Hans de Jong

Party Invitation パーティー招待状

Design Firm／デザイン
USA 1996
CL, DF: White Plus
CD: Trina Nuovo
D, P: Barbara Chan
CW: Daryl Forkell

Exhibition Invitation
展示会招待状

Apparel Manufacturers Association／
アパレル工業組合
Japan 1997
CL: 東京婦人子供服工業組合
Tokyo Women's & Children's Wear Manufacturers Association
CD, AD: 淺葉 勝　Katsu Asano
D: 米澤帛笑　Kinue Yonezawa
DF: ㈱アーサー・ハンドレッド・カンパニー　ASA 100 Company

Dance Show Invitation
ダンス公演招待状

University／大学
Spain 1996
CL: Universitat Autonoma de Barcelona
CD, D: Lluis Jubert
AD: Ramon Enrich
P: Ramon Pallares
CW, DF: Espai Grafic

Movie Invitation 映画招待状

Movie Theatre／映画館
Switzerland 1996
CL: Kinos Aarau
AD, D: Lucia Frey
DF: Wild & Frey, Agentur für Design

Exhibition Invitation
展示会招待状

Culture Center／文化施設
Spain 1996
CL: ATLAS
CD, D: Lluis Jubert
AD: Ramon Enrich
P: Ramon Pallares
CW, DF: Espai Grafic

Party Invitation
パーティー招待状

Personal／個人
Netherlands 1996
CL: Dick Sikkes
CD, AD, D: Wout de Vringer
CW: Dick Sikkes
DF: Faydherbe / de Vringer

The Management and Staff
of
Hongkong Land Limited
cordially invites

....

....

to the Ceremonial Switch-on
of the Festive Illuminations
by Mrs Percy Weatherall
on Friday, 8th December 1995, at 6.00pm
at The Landmark Atrium, Hong Kong

Cocktails 5.30pm-7.30pm

R.S.V.P. 2842-8459

INVITATION

Party Invitation パーティー招待状

Publisher／出版
France 1996
CL: Première
AD: Marie-Laure Cruz & Agnès Cruz
I: Emmanuel Pierre
Illustrator's Agent in Japan: CWC

Festival & Auction Invitation
フェスティバル＆オークション招待状

School／学校
USA 1993
CL: The Beginnings Nursery School
AD, D: Susan Hochbaum
I: Steven Guarnaccia

P.62 Ceremony Invitation
セレモニー招待状

Land Development Company／土地開発
Hong Kong 1995
CL: The Hongkong Land Group Ltd.
CD, AD: Kan Tai-keung
AD: Freeman Lau Siu Hong
D: Man Lee Chi Man
DF: Kan & Lau Design Consultants

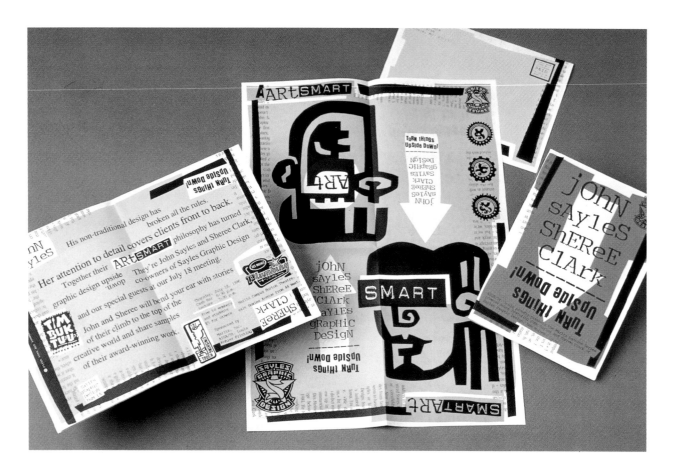

Speech Invitation
スピーチ招待状

Professional Organization／同業者協会
USA 1996
CL: St. Louis AIGA
CD, AD, D, I: John Sayles
D: Jennifer Elliott
CW: Kristin Lennert
DF: Sayles Graphic Design

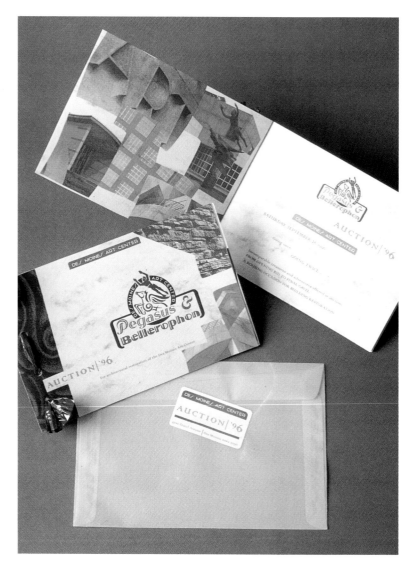

Dinner & Auction Invitation
ディナー＆オークション招待状

Art Museum／美術館
USA 1996
CL: Des Moines Art Center
CD, AD, D, I: John Sayles
D: Jennifer Elliott
P: Bill Nellans
CW: Annie Meacham
DF: Sayles Graphic Design

1 *Party Invitation*
パーティー招待状

University／大学
Spain 1996
CL: Universitat de Barcelona
CD, D: Lluis Jubert
AD, D: Ramon Enrich
P: Ramon Pallares
CW, DF: Espai Grafic

2 *Music Festival Invitation*
音楽祭招待状

City Hall／市民ホール
Spain 1994
CL: Ajuntament D'Igualada
CD, D: Lluis Jubert
AD: Ramon Enrich
P: Ramon Pallares
CW, DF: Espai Grafic

3 *Dance Invitation*
ダンス招待状

Theater／劇場
Netherlands 1996
CL: Maas Theater
CD, AD, D: Limage Dangereuse
P: Hans de Jong

Invitation to View New Collection
コレクション招待状

Shoe Company／靴製造販売
Netherlands 1995
CL: Sacha Shoes
CD: Bert Termeer
AD, D: Petra Janssen / Edwin Vollebergh
P: René Van Der Hulst
I, DF: Studio Boot

Invitation to
View New Collection
コレクション招待状

Shoe Company／靴製造販売
Netherlands 1995
CL: Sacha Shoes
CD: Bert Ter Meer
AD, D: Petra Janssen /
Edwin Vollebergh
P: René Van Der Hulst
I, DF: Studio Boot

Housewarming Invitation
引越パーティー招待状

Personal／個人
USA 1996
CL: Ross Crowe / Scott Hartle
AD, D, CW: Ellie Leacock
DF: Art Stuff

GETTING 26 AND ALL EXITED.

STEFAN SAGMEISTER
9 CLINTON STREET
NEW YORK, NEW YORK 10002

P.68 *Birthday Party Invitation*
誕生日会招待状

Designer／デザイナー
USA 1994
CL: Stefan Sagmeister
CD, AD, D, I, CW: Stefan Sagmeister
DF: Sagmeister Inc.

Ceremony Invitation
セレモニー招待状

Land Development Company／土地開発
Hong Kong 1994
CL: The Hongkong Land Group Ltd.
CD: Kan Tai-keung
AD, D: Clement Yick Tat Wa
DF: Kan & Lau Design Consultants

Bar Mitzvah Invitation
バルミツヴァ招待状

Graphic Designer／グラフィックデザイナー
Canada 1996
CL: Roslyn Eskind
AD, D: Roslyn Eskind
D: Nicola Lyon
DF: Eskind Waddell

バルミツヴァはユダヤ教の男性の成人式。
A bar mitzvah is a Jewish ceremony in which
a 13-year-old boy becomes recognized as an adult.

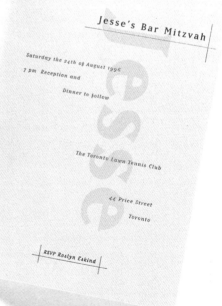

Conference Invitation
会議招待状

Union／組合
Italy 1997
CL: Actors Union
AD: Antonio Romano
D, I: Fabio Finocchioli
I: Stefania Cinquini
P: Giuseppe Maria Fadda
Project Manager: Monica Soli Meno
DF: AREA-Strategic Design

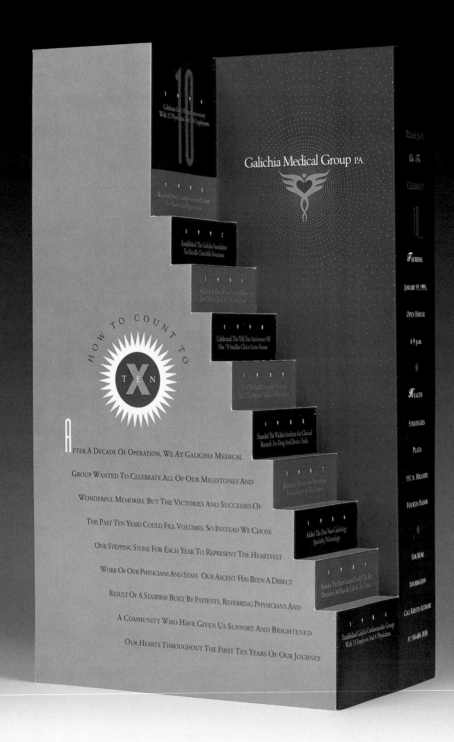

10th Anniversary Invitation
10周年記念招待状

Medical Group／医療団体
USA 1995
CL: Galichia Medical Group
CD, AD, D: Sonia Greteman
AD, D: James Strange
DF: Greteman Group

1 *Convention Invitation*
会議招待状

Jet Manufacturer／ジェットエンジン製造
USA 1996
CL: Learjet Inc.
CD, AD, D, I: Sonia Greteman
D: James Strange
DF: Greteman Group

2 *Convention Invitation*
会議招待状

Jet Manufacturer／ジェットエンジン製造
USA 1995
CL: Learjet Inc.
CD, AD, D: Sonia Greteman
AD, D, I: James Strange
DF: Greteman Group

Birthday Party Invitation
誕生日会招待状

Personal／個人
Austria 1996
CL: Oswald Brunner
CD, D: Kurt Dornig
I: John Gilbert
CW: Hermann Brändle
DF: Kurt Dornig Grafik-Design &
Illustration

Convention Invitation
会議招待状

Jet Manufacturer／ジェットエンジン製造
USA 1994
CL: Learjet Inc.
CD, AD, D: Sonia Greteman
AD, D, I: James Strange
DF: Greteman Group

Dinner Invitation
ディナー招待状

University／大学
Spain 1996
CL: Seruei D'Activitat Fisica
CD, D: Lluis Jubert
AD: Ramon Enrich
P: Ramon Pallares
CW, DF: Espai Grafic

Party Invitation
パーティー招待状

Architecture & Design／
建築設計, デザイン
USA 1996
CL: NBBJ
D: Amy Lam
DF: NBBJ Graphic Design

Party Invitation
パーティー招待状

Property Management／ビル管理
USA 1996
CL: Columbia Seafirst
D: Daniel R. Smith
DF: NBBJ Graphic Design

Party Invitation
パーティー招待状

Design Firm／デザイン
Fashion Importer & Retailer／
インポートファッション販売
Japan 1996
CL: ㈱アルトカンポ ALTO CAMPO COMPANY
AD: 高畑 小百合 Sayuri Takahata
D: 高畑三穂 Miho Takahata／
松井 薫 Kaoru Matsui／久保憲子 Noriko Kubo／
外崎和子 Kazuko Tonosaki／
木村智子 Tomoko Kimura／韓 寿江 Sugang Kan

Meeting Announcement
会議案内状

Newspaper／新聞社
Japan 1995
CL: 関西ジャーナル社 Kansai Journal
CD: 折目允亮 Masaaki Orime
D: 清水正行 Masayuki Shimizu
I: 川瀬奈歩 Naho Kawase

HOW ABOUT YOU?

How about you? 9.27 wed. 4pm~7pm Nite Cafe Qoo

KANSAI JOURNAL 15

ご出席
ご欠席
ご芳名　ご同伴　名
住所
所属
電話番号

CHAMPAGNER PARTY bei Sagmeister

CHAMPAGNER PARTY bei Sagmeister

1

2

1,2 Party Invitation
パーティー招待状

Women's Fashion Retail／婦人服小売
Austria 1996 (2) / 1997 (1)
CL: Martin Sagmeister
CD, AD: Stefan Sagmeister
D: Hjalti Karlson (1) / Veronica Oh (2)
D, I: Alexander Pohl (1) / Heike Reinsch (2)
P: Tom Schierlitz
CW: Martin Sagmeister
DF: Sagmeister Inc.

1 *Exhibition Invitation*
展示会招待状

Apparel Manufacturers Association／
アパレル工業組合
Japan 1997
CL: 東京婦人子供服工業組合 Tokyo Women's &
Children's Wear Manufacturers Association
CD, AD: 淺葉 勝 Katsu Asano
D: 米澤帛笑 Kinue Yonezawa
P: 福島 力 Liki Fukushima
DF: ㈱アーサー・ハンドレッド・カンパニー
ASA 100 Company

2

1

2 *Party Invitation*
パーティー招待状

Property Management／ビル管理
USA 1995
CL: Columbia Seafirst
D: Stefanie Choi
DF: NBBJ Graphic Design

3 *Event Invitation*
イベント招待状

Chamber of Commerce Support Group／
商業会議所サポート団体
USA 1997
CL: San Francisco Business Arts Council
CD, AD, D: Mark Sackett
D: Wayne Sakamoto / James Sakamoto
I: Eric Siemens
DF: Sackett Design Associates

3

Dinner Invitation
ディナー招待状

Non-profit Organization／非営利団体
USA 1995
CL: Gay & Lesbian Task Force
CD: Tibor Kalman
AD, D: Stefan Sagmeister
D: Tom Walker
CW: Cee Brown
DF: M & Co., New York

ゲイとレズビアンのための活動グループ主催のディナー
パーティーへの招待状
Invitation to a dinner party organized by a Gay and
Lesbian rights group.

Opening Invitation
オープニング招待状

Coffee Bar and Restaurant／レストラン
USA 1995
CL: Timbuktuu Coffee Bar
CD, AD, D, I: John Sayles
D: Jennifer Elliott
CW: Annie Meacham
DF: Sayles Graphic Design

1

Wir heiraten.
Wolfram und Sonja
am 16. Juni um 14.30
in der Loretokapelle
in Lustenau.

Am Abend gibt's
ein Festessen
im Gasthof Schiffle
dazu laden wir
herzlich ein.

Mona zeichnet
den Bräutigam...

2

Renate & Reini heiraten
am 26. Mai 1995 um 16.00 Uhr
in der Kirche Wattenegg.

1,2 *Wedding Invitation*
結婚式招待状

Personal／個人
Austria 1995
CL: Sonja & Wolfram Greber (1) /
Renate & Reini (2)
CD: Sigi Ramoser
I: Mona & Sarah (2)

Wedding Invitation
結婚式招待状

Personal／個人
Switzerland 1995
CL: Dona Bertarelli
CD, AD, D, DF: Oscar Ribes

Wedding Invitation
結婚式招待状

Personal／個人
Austria 1997
CL: Birgit & Andreas Ölz
CD, D, I: Kurt Dornig
DF: Kurt Dornig Grafik-Design & Illustration

Wedding Invitation
結婚式招待状

Personal／個人
Japan 1995
CL, DF: ワンストローク One Stroke Co., Ltd.
AD, D: 駒形克己 Katsumi Komagata
D: 駒形みち子 Michiko Komagata
D: 石嶋亜紀 Aki Ishijima

Wedding Invitation
結婚式招待状

Personal／個人
Japan 1994
CL: 長嶋寛明 Hiroaki Nagashima
AD, D: 駒形克己 Katsumi Komagata
DF: ワンストローク One Stroke Co., Ltd.

Wedding Invitation
結婚式招待状

Personal／個人
Australia 1995
CL: Teresa Fernandez
CD, D: Karel Wöhlnick
CW: Teresa Fernandez
DF: Wöhlnick Design

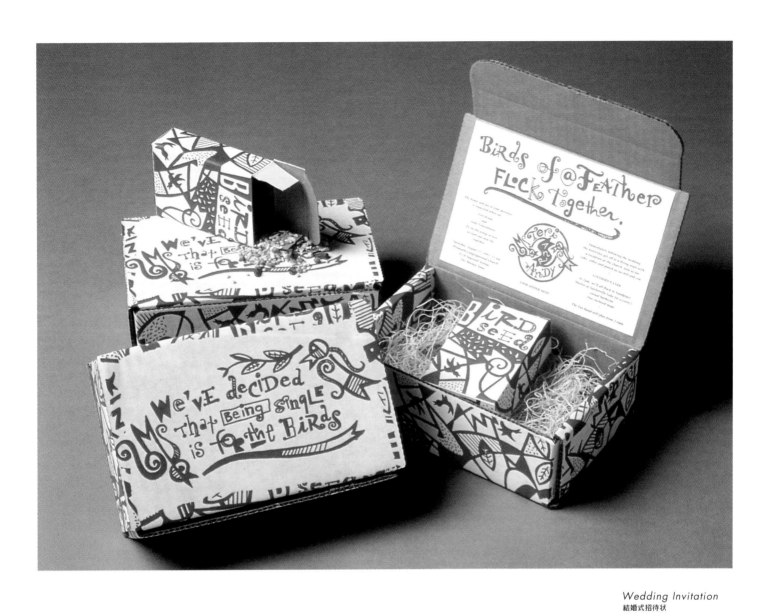

Wedding Invitation
結婚式招待状

Personal／個人
USA 1993
CL: Teri & Andy TeBockhorst
CD, AD, D, I: John Sayles
CW: Teri Wood
DF: Sayles Graphic Design

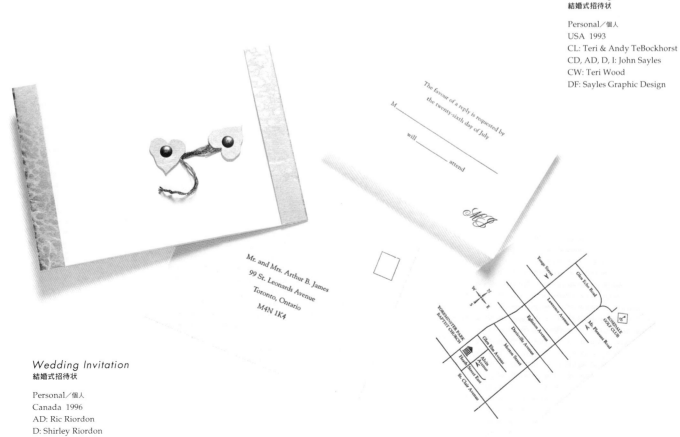

Wedding Invitation
結婚式招待状

Personal／個人
Canada 1996
AD: Ric Riordon
D: Shirley Riordon
DF: The Riordon Design Group Inc.

083

Wedding Invitation
結婚式招待状

Personal／個人 Japan 1994
CL: 濱岡 純 Jun Hamaoka ／ 佐藤真理子 Mariko Sato
AD, D: 吉野修平 Shuhei Yoshino
DF: ㈲ヨシノデザインオフィス Yoshino Design Office Inc.

Wedding Invitation
結婚式招待状

Personal／個人
Austria 1995
CL: Karin & Heiner Messerle
CD: Sigi Ramoser

Wedding Invitation
結婚式招待状

Architect／建築家
Japan 1995
CL: 田代敦久 Atsuhisa Tashiro
CD, AD, D, I, CW: 森島紘史 Hiroshi Morishima
DF: タイム・スペース・アート㈱
Time-Space-Art Inc.

Wedding Invitation
結婚式招待状

Personal／個人
Germany 1995
CL: Konstantin Jacoby
D, I: Johannes Erler
D, P: Uwe Melichar
DF: Factor Design

Wedding Invitation
結婚式招待状

Personal／個人
USA 1994
CL: Laurie Cropp / Steven Groves
CD, AD, D: Ted Groves
DF: Myriad Inc.

Wedding Invitation
結婚式招待状

Personal／個人
Japan 1995
CD, AD, D, DF: トゥーループ・グラフィックス
TOLOOP graphics

Wedding Invitation 結婚式招待状

Personal／個人 USA 1997
CL: Peter & Elizabeth Lord
CD, AD, D: Peter Lord   D: Elizabeth Carluccio Lord

Wedding Invitation
結婚式招待状

Personal／個人
Australia 1994
CL: Anna & David Eagle
CD, AD, D: John Spatchurst
DF: Spatchurst Design

Wedding Invitation
結婚式招待状

Personal／個人
France 1996
CL: Ludovic & Velérie Rio
CD, AD, D, I: Pascale Bortolotti

Wedding Invitation
結婚式招待状

Graphic Designer／グラフィックデザイナー
Mexico 1996
CL, CD, AD, D: Patrick Burgeff

Wedding Invitation
結婚式招待状

Personal／個人
Yugoslavia 1993
CD, AD, D, CW, DF: Škart Group
I: Goran Patlejh

INVITATIONS

1 *Wedding Invitation*
結婚式招待状

Personal／個人
Hong Kong 1996
CL: Arcadia & Robert
CD: Steve Lau
AD, D, I: Shirley Kong
DF: Twice Graphics

2 *Wedding Invitation*
結婚式招待状

Personal／個人
Hong Kong 1996
CL: Eva & David
CD, AD, D, I: Steve Lau
D, I: Shirley Kong
CW: Lee Wolter Co., Ltd.
DF: Twice Graphics

Wedding Invitation
結婚式招待状

Personal／個人
USA 1992
CL: Matt & Angela Sackett
CD, AD, D: Mark Sackett
D: Wayne Sakamoto / James Sakamoto
DF: Sackett Design Associates

Wedding Invitation
結婚式招待状

Design Firm／デザイン
Hong Kong 1995
CL, DF: J & J Graphic Design Co.
CD, AD: Jacklyn Chow
D, I: Jimmy Lo
P: Eric Chow
CW: Chow Lai Ming

1,3 Wedding Invitation
結婚式招待状

Personal／個人
Germany 1997
CL: Lisa Buskamp
D: Daniel Bastian
DF: Form Fünf

1

2

2 Wedding Invitation
結婚式招待状

Personal／個人
Yugoslavia 1996
CL: Zoran Ivanović
CD, AD, D, CW, DF: Škart Group

3

P.91
1 Exhibition Invitation
展示会招待状

Art Gallery／ギャラリー
Japan 1997
CL: ギャラリィ・ロケット art laboratory Rocket
CD, CW: 沼田元氣 Genqui Numata
AD: 藤本やすし Yasushi Fujimoto
D: キャップ（李＆青木） CAP(Lee & Aoki)

2 Exhibition Invitation
展示会招待状

Art Gallery／ギャラリー
Netherlands 1995
CL: Centrum Beeldende Kunst Dordrecht
CD, AD, D: Wout de Vringer
DF: Faydherbe / de Vringer

3 Exhibition Opening Invitation
展示会オープニング招待状

Museum／美術館
USA 1994
CL: The Computer Museum
CD, AD, D, CW: Ted Groves
DF: Myriad Inc.

Genqui
Numata
Exhibition

Souvenir
shop of
Readymade or
Numagen's
Rose therapy
1997.07.11~07.23
at art laboratory
ROCKET

沼田元氣個展

GRAPH

Souvenir shop
of
Readymade
or
Numagen's
Rose therapy

1

2

3

Het Nederlandse Sieraad

08
07
95
'm
06
08
93

Guests unable to attend the Boston
opening may attend receptions at either
of two networked sites:

Sprint Applied Technology Center,
Washington D.C.

Sprint Applied Technology Center,
San Mateo, California
(Event starts at 3:30pst)

THE NETWORKED PLANET

Traveling the Information Highway

A Permanent Exhibit at
The Computer Museum

Here's your chance
to have the entire world
at your fingertips.

Design Exhibition Invitation
デザイン展招待状

Educational Institute／教育機関
Singapore 1997
CL: School of Design, Temasek Polytechnic
CD, AD, D, I: Hon Soo Tien

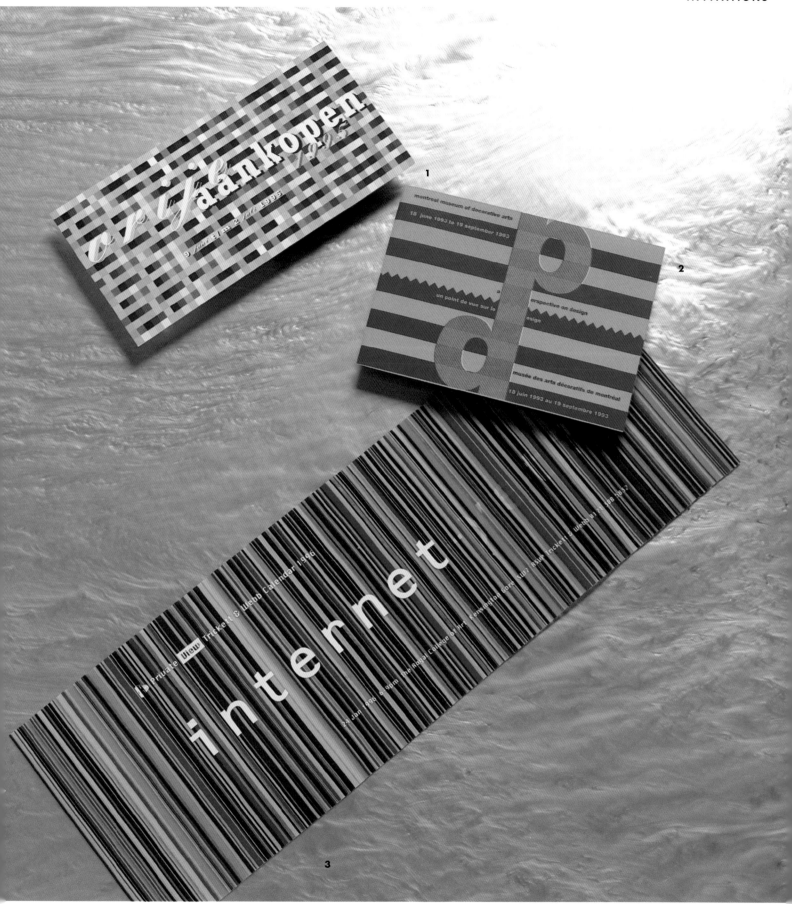

1 *Exhibition Invitation*
展示会招待状

Art Gallery／ギャラリー
Netherlands 1995
CL: Centrum Beeldende Kunst Dordrecht
CD, AD, D: Wout de Vringer
DF: Faydherbe / de Vringer

2 *Exhibition Invitation*
展示会招待状

Museum／美術館
Canada 1993
CL: Montreal Museum of Decorative Arts
CD, AD, D: Takaaki Matsumoto
DF: Matsumoto, Inc.

3 *Exhibition Invitation*
展示会招待状

Designers／デザイナー
UK 1996
CL, DF: Trickett & Webb Ltd.
CD, D: Brian Webb / Lynn Trickett
D: Colin Gifforo

Fair Invitation
イベント招待状

Professional Organization／同業者協会
USA 1997
CL: American Institute of Graphic Arts /
New York
D: J. Graham Hanson
CW: Leslie Adler
DF: J. Graham Hanson Design

Exhibition Invitation
展示会招待状

Artist／アーティスト
Netherlands 1995
CL, CD, P: Hans Van Bentem
AD, D: Wout de Vringer
DF: Faydherbe / de Vringer

1,2 *Exhibition Invitation*
展示会案内

Eyeglass Maker／メガネメーカー (1)
Apparel Maker／アパレルメーカー (2)
Japan 1994
CL: オプトインター㈱ Opto Inter Co., Ltd. (1) /
バルーインク Barreaux Inc. (2)
CD, AD: 淺埜 勝 Katsu Asano
AD, D: 宇治智子 Tomoko Uji (1)
D: 米澤帛笑 Kinue Yonezawa
DF: ㈱アーサー・ハンドレッド・カンパニー
ASA 100 Company

1

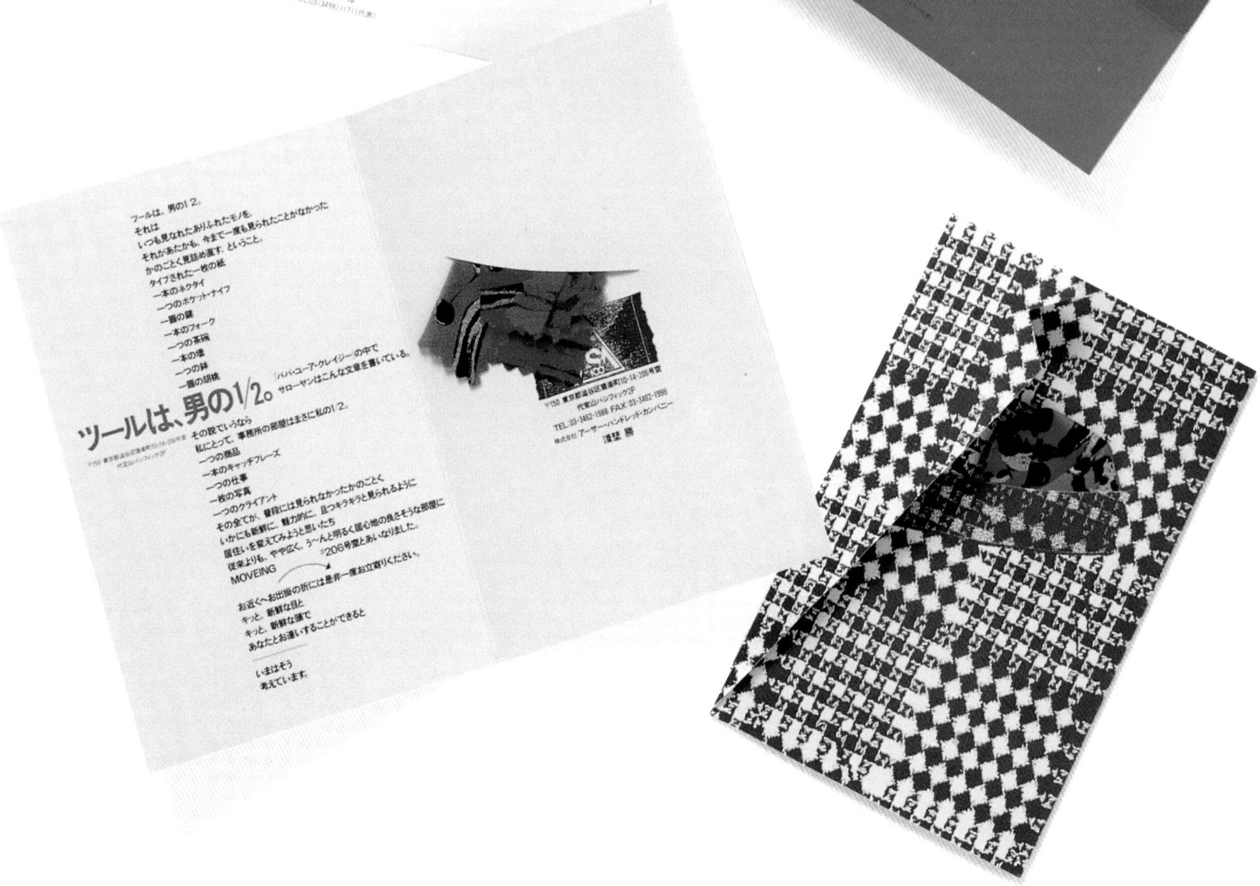

2

1 *Art Exhibition Opening Invitation*
展示会オープニング招待状

Art Gallery／ギャラリー
Mexico 1995
CL: Galeria Arte Contemporaneo
CD, AD, D: Joanna Slazak
CD: Antonio Sanchez

1

hector
bialostozky

carlos
julio
molina

daniel
guzman

2

Ramon Enrich

3

RAMON ENRICH MALEREI

Architektur und Landschaft

2,3 *Exhibition Invitation*
展示会招待状

Art Gallery／ギャラリー (2)
Art Center／アートセンター (3)
Spain 1996
CL: H₂O Barcelona (2) /
Kuntslerhaus Mousonturm (3)
CD, D: Lluis Jubert
AD: Ramon Enrich
P: Ramon Pallares
CW, DF: Espai Grafic

1 *Exhibition Invitation*
展示会招待状

Publicity Agency／広告
Spain 1995
CL: Sala Tandem DDB & Publivia
CD, D, CW: Gabriel Espi
P, CW: Roger Velazquez

2,4 *Exhibition Invitation*
展示会招待状

Photographer／フォトグラファー (2)
University／大学 (4)
Spain 1996 (2) / 1997 (4)
CL: Roger Velazquez (2) /
Universitat de Barcelona (4)
CD, D: Lluis Jubert
AD: Ramon Enrich
P: Roger Velazquez (2) / Ramon Pallares (4)
CW, DF: Espai Grafic

3 *Exhibition Invitation*
展示会招待状

Art Gallery／ギャラリー
Netherlands 1994
CL: Centrum Beeldende Kunst Dordrecht
CD, AD, D: Wout de Vringer
DF: Faydherbe / de Vringer

097

1 *Exhibition Opening Invitation*
展示会オープニング招待状

Four-year Non-profit Art College／大学
USA 1997
CL: Art Center College of Design
CD: Stuart I. Frolick
AD, D: Darin Beaman
D: Greg Chinn
DF: Art Center College of Design-Design Office

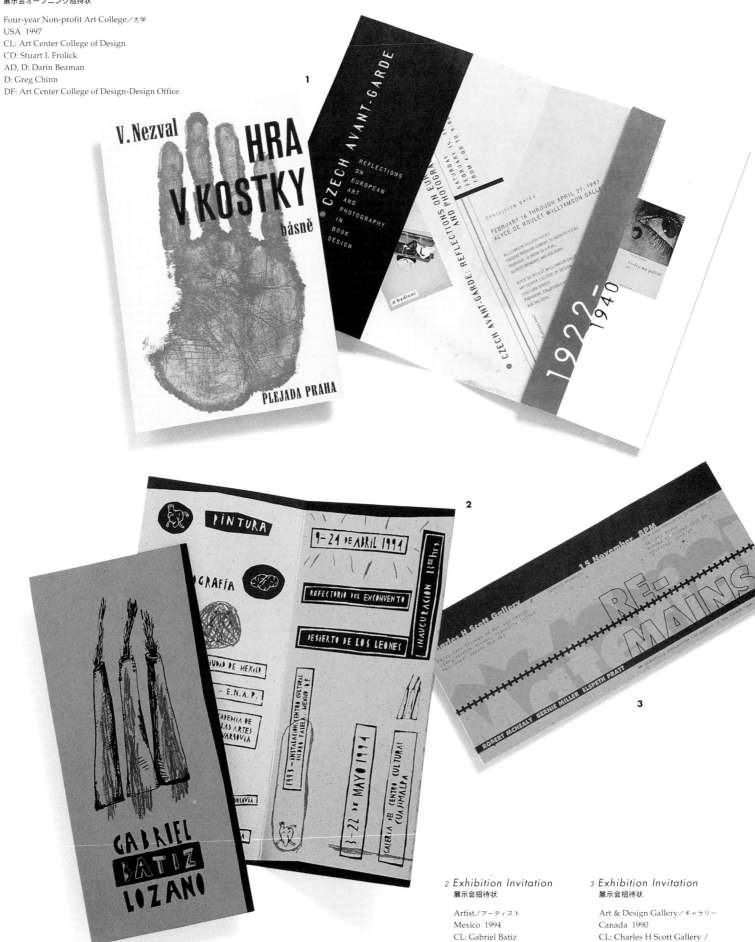

2 *Exhibition Invitation*
展示会招待状

Artist／アーティスト
Mexico 1994
CL: Gabriel Batiz
CD, AD, D, I: Joanna Slazak

3 *Exhibition Invitation*
展示会招待状

Art & Design Gallery／ギャラリー
Canada 1990
CL: Charles H Scott Gallery ／
Greg Bellerby, Curator
CD, D: Terrance Zacharko
CW: Greg Bellerby
DF: Zacharko Design Partnership

1 *Exhibition Invitation*
展示会招待状

Art & Design Gallery／ギャラリー
Canada 1990
CL: Charles H Scott Gallery /
Greg Bellerby, Curator
CD, D: Terrance Zacharko
CW: Greg Bellerby
DF: Zacharko Design Partnership

2,3 *Exhibition Invitation*
展示会招待状

Art Gallery／ギャラリー
Netherlands 1994
CL: Unica & Replica (2) /
Centrum Beeldende Kunst Dordrecht (3)
CD, AD, D: Wout de Vringer
DF: Faydherbe / de Vringer

1 *Exhibition Invitation* 展示会招待状
Designers／デザイナー　UK　1995　CL, DF: Trickett & Webb Ltd.　CD, D: Brian Webb / Lynn Trickett　D: Colin Gifford

2 *Invitation to View New Collection* コレクション招待状
Fashion Designer／ファッションデザイナー　Japan　1993　CL: Nigel Curtiss Co., Ltd.　D, DF: Susan Moriguchi

1 *Exhibition Invitation* 展示会招待状
Designers／デザイナー　UK　1997　CL, DF: Trickett & Webb Ltd.　CD, D: Brian Webb / Lynn Trickett　D: Matt Baxter　I: Andy Bridge

2 *Exhibition Invitation* 展示会招待状
Photographers' Association／写真家協会　Hong Kong　1993　CL: Hong Kong Institute of Professional Photographers　CD: Kan Tai-keung　AD, D: Freeman Lau Siu Hong
D: Janet Lau Man Ying　P: C K Wong　DF: Kan & Lau Design Consultants

1 *Exhibition Invitation*
展示会招待状

2 *Exhibition Invitation*
展示会招待状

Design Firm／デザイン
Hong Kong 1996
CL, DF: Kan & Lau Design Consultants
CD, AD, D, Ink Painting: Kan Tai-keung
D: Chau So Hing
P: C. K. Wong
I: John Tam Mo Fai

Education Institute／教育機関
Hong Kong 1996
CL: The Centre for Int'l Arts Education
Exchange of the Central Institute of Fine Arts
CD, AD, D: Kan Tai-keung
P: C. K. Wong
DF: Kan & Lau Design Consultants

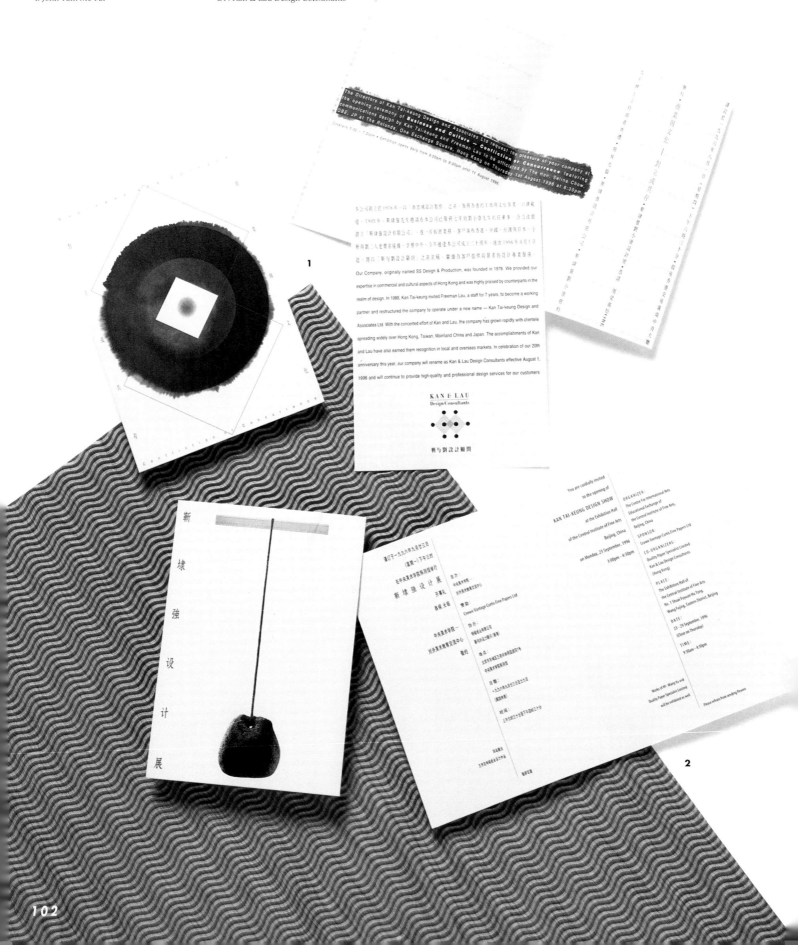

1 *Exhibition Invitation*
展示会招待状

Graphic Designers Association／
グラフィックデザイナー協会
Hong Kong 1996
CL: Hong Kong Designers Association
AD, D: Freeman Lau Siu Hong
D: Fanny Ng Wai Han
DF: Kan & Lau Design Consultants

2 *Exhibition Invitation*
展示会招待状

Design Firm／デザイン
Japan 1994
CL, D, DF: ミュゼ Musée
AD: 福田隆志 Takashi Fukuda

3 *Exhibition Invitation*
展示会招待状

Graphic Designer／グラフィックデザイナー
Taiwan 1997
CL, CD, AD, D: Leslie Chan Wing Kei
DF: Leslie Chan Design Co., Ltd.

Exhibition Invitation
展覧会案内状

Foundation／財団
Japan 1997
CL: (財) 児童育成協会 こどもの城
National Children's Castle
AD, D: 駒形克己 Katsumi Komagata
DF: ワンストローク One Stroke Co., Ltd.

Exhibition Invitation
展示会案内

Shoe Manufacturer／靴製造販売
Japan 1997
CL: ㈱キサ KISSA Co., Ltd.
AD: 養父正一 Shoichi Yabu
D: 松田英之 Hideyuki Matsuda
I: 高田喜佐 Kisa Takada
DF: Eye Some Design

Exhibition Invitation
展示会招待状

Apparel Maker／アパレルメーカー
Japan 1997
CL: イッセイミヤケ Issey Miyake
AD: 勝井三雄 Mitsuo Katsui

Exhibition Invitation
展示会案内状

Paper Manufacturer／製紙
Japan 1996
CL: 特種製紙㈱
Tokushu Paper Manufacturing Co., Ltd.
AD, D: 駒形克己 Katsumi Komagata
DF: ワンストローク One Stroke Co., Ltd.

Designatorium Timepieces
ロス・ミクブライドの12の時計
OPENING PARTY
Friday, April 18, 1997
from 7:00p.m. to 8:30p.m.
at the Living Design Gallery
Shinjuku Park Tower, Ozone 6F
for information call: 03-3470-6526

Exhibition Opening Invitation
展示会オープニング案内状

Artist／アーティスト
Japan 1997
CL, CD, AD, D, I: Ross McBride
CW: 川上典子 Noriko Kawakami
DF: デザイナトリウム Designatorium

seasonal greetings

SAM GOES TO HOLLYWOOD
AWARDS
11.11.96
TEN

christmas cards

new year cards   others

Christmas クリスマス

Design Firm／デザイン
Spain 1996
CL, CW, DF: Espai Grafic
CD, D: Lluis Jubert
AD, D: Ramon Enrich
P, CW: Roger Velazquez

1 *Christmas* クリスマス

Auto Manufacturer／自動車メーカー
Japan 1994
CL: トヨタ Toyota
CD: 天野 知恵美 Chiemi Amano
AD: 清水節江 Setsue Shimizu
CW: こしみず幸三 Kozo Koshimizu

カードを開くと天使が飛び出すしかけになっている。
As the card is opened, an angel flies out.

2 *Christmas* クリスマス

Apparel Maker／アパレルメーカー
Japan 1995
CL: ㈱アルファベット パステル
Alphabet Pastel Co., Ltd.
D: 室谷真澄 Masumi Muroya

3 *Christmas* クリスマス

Design Firm／デザイン
Italy 1996
CL: Kuni-Graphic Design Company
CD: Barbara Cuniberti
AD, D: Danila Golfieri

Christmas クリスマス

Women's Clothing Retailer／婦人服小売
USA 1993
CL: Aspen Traders
CD, AD, D: Sonia Greteman
D: Karen Hogan
DF: Greteman Group

1

1,2 Christmas クリスマス

Design Firm／デザイン
USA 1994 (2) / 1995 (1)
CL, DF: Julia Tam Design
CD, AD, D, I: Julia Chong Tam

2

Merry
Christmas

PAPER POWER

CHARTERED PAPER PRODUCT DESIGN
CREATIVE PAPER ENGINEERING DE

© 1994 PAPER POWER

1

2

1,2 *Christmas* クリスマス

Paper Product Design／ペーパープロダクトデザイン
UK 1994 (1) / 1996 (2)
CL, DF: Paper Power
CD, AD, D: Lyn Hourahine

1 *Christmas*　クリスマス

Music Producers／音楽プロダクション
UK 1996
CL: P+E Music Ltd.
CD, AD, D: Paula Benson / Paul West
D: Lisa Smith
DF: Form

2,3 *Christmas*　クリスマス

Music Producers／音楽プロダクション
UK 1992 (2) / 1993 (3)
CL: Chaps
CD, AD, D: Paula Benson / Paul West
DF: Form

1

2

CHAPS

★
WISHING YOU A
MERRY CHRISTMAS AND
A HAPPY '94

FROM PHIL AND IAN

3

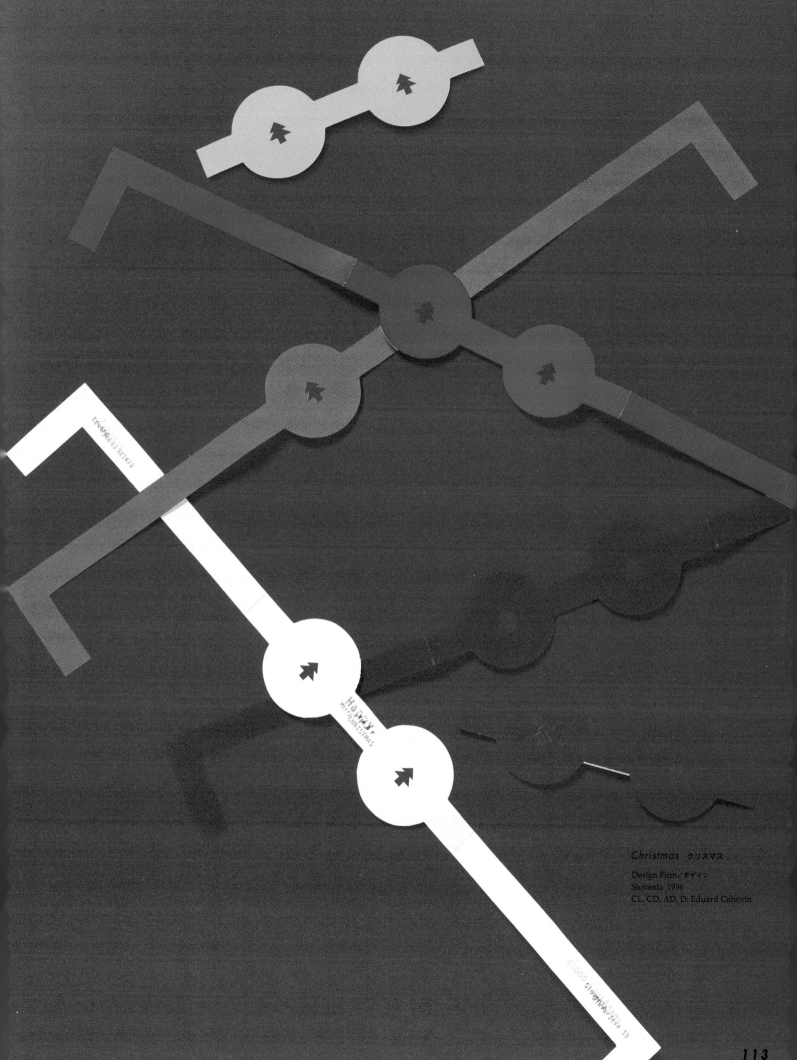

Christmas クリスマス

Design Firm/デザイン
Slovenia 1996
CL, CD, AD, D: Eduard Cehovin

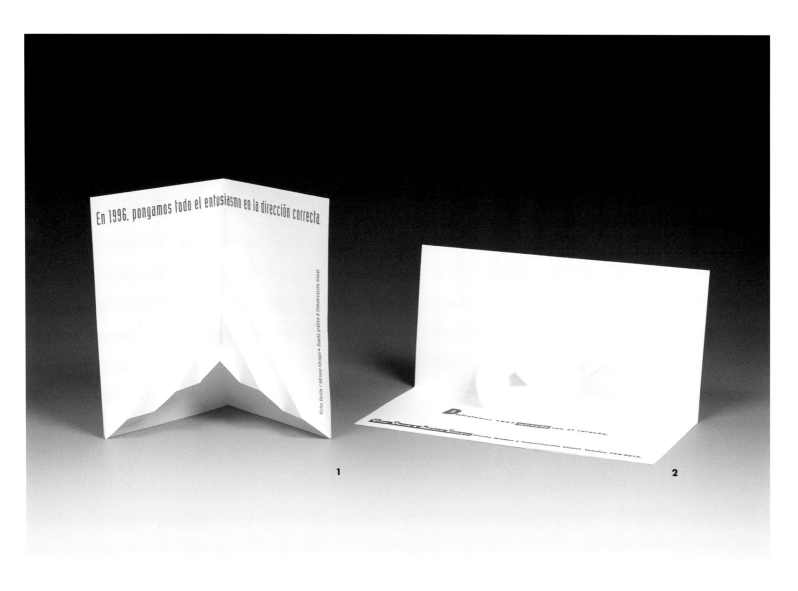

En 1996, pongamos todo el entusiasmo en la dirección correcta.

1

2

1,2 **New Year** 年賀状

Design Firm／デザイン
Argentina 1995 (1) / 1996 (2)
CL, DF: Victor Garcia / Adriana Ellinger
CD, AD, D, CW: Victor Garcia

Wishing you A Merry X'mas
and
A Happy New Year.

Deseamos que sus mejores proyectos lleguen a buen puerto. ¡Felicidades!

PAGLIETTINI

3

3 **New Year** 年賀状

River Dredging Company／浚渫業
Argentina 1996
CL: Pagliettini Dragados
CD, AD, D, CW: Victor Garcia
DF: Victor Garcia Deseño Grafico

4 **Christmas** クリスマス

Design Firm／デザイン
Japan 1997
CL: アール・ビー・エム・デザインスタジオ
r. p. m. Design Studio
CD: 高橋洋一 Yoichi Takahashi

4

Christmas クリスマス

Paper Product Design／ペーパープロダクトデザイン
UK 1995
CL, DF: Paper Power
CD, AD, D: Lyn Hourahine

Christmas クリスマス

Design Firm／デザイン
USA 1994
CL, DF: Wang & Williams
CD, AD, D, I: Ming Wang
CD, D, CW: Denise Williams

Christmas クリスマス

Design Firm／デザイン
Hong Kong 1995
CL, CW, DF: Twice Graphics
CD, AD: Steve Lau
D, I: Alex Leung

Christmas クリスマス

Personal／個人
Austria 1996
CL: Eugen Wenin
CD: Sigi Ramoser

Christmas クリスマス

Photo Studio／フォトスタジオ
Austria 1994
CL, P: S. F. &. H.
CD, AD, D: Sigi Ramoser
DF: Atelier für Text und Gestaltung

Christmas　クリスマス

Gas Utility／ガス
USA　1995
CL: Enron Corporation
CD, AD, D: Eric Rickabaugh
I: Children of Enron Employees
DF: Rickabaugh Graphics

Christmas　クリスマス

Design Firm／デザイン
USA　1996
CL, DF: Rickabaugh Graphics
AD: Eric Rickabaugh
D, I, CW: Dean DeShetler

Christmas　クリスマス

Gas Utility／ガス
USA　1996
CL: Enron, Capitol & Trade Resources
AD: Eric Rickabaugh　D: Dean DeShetler
I: Children of Enron Associates
CW: Enron　DF: Rickabaugh Graphics

Christmas クリスマス

Design Studio／デザイン
Spain 1995
CL, DF: Espai Grafic
CD, CW: Enrich / Jubert
CD, P, CW: Roger Velazquez

パラパラとページをめくると写真が動いて見える。
Flip the pages and the photos will appear to become animated.

1

1 *Christmas* クリスマス

Design Firm／デザイン
Hong Kong 1997
CL, DF: Teamwork Design Ltd.
CD, AD, D, I: Gary Tam
D, I: Joey Ong

3

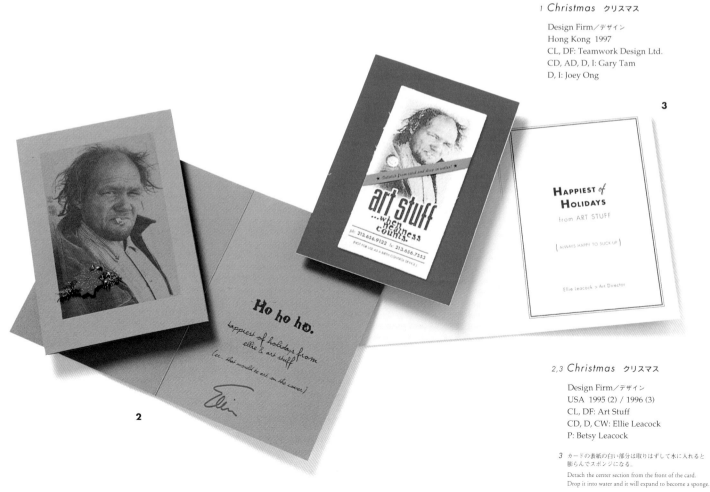

2

2,3 *Christmas* クリスマス

Design Firm／デザイン
USA 1995 (2) / 1996 (3)
CL, DF: Art Stuff
CD, D, CW: Ellie Leacock
P: Betsy Leacock

3 カードの表紙の白い部分は取りはずして水に入れると
膨らんでスポンジになる。
Detach the center section from the front of the card.
Drop it into water and it will expand to become a sponge.

Christmas　クリスマス

Design Consultants／デザインコンサルタント
Australia 1995
CL, DF: Sophie Bartho & Associates
CD, AD, D: Sophie Bartho

Christmas　クリスマス

Consultant／コンサルタント
Australia 1996
CL ,DF: Poagi
CD: David Bland
D: Timothy Murphy

Christmas　クリスマス

Apparel Maker／アパレルメーカー
Australia 1995
CL: Image Clothing
CD: Sophie Bartho
D: Naaz Kerr
DF: Sophie Bartho & Associates

Christmas　クリスマス

Design Consultants／デザインコンサルタント
Australia 1994
CL, DF: Sophie Bartho & Associates
CD, AD, D: Sophie Bartho

カードに本物のビスケットが付いている。
A real biscuit is attached to the card.

New Year 年賀状

Design Firm／デザイン
Hong Kong 1994
CL, CW, DF: Twice Graphics
CD, AD: Steve Lau
D, I: Danny Chan

Christmas クリスマス

Paper Merchant／製紙卸
Australia 1996
CL: The Paper House
CD, AD, D, I: David Lancashire
DF: David Lancashire Design

1 *Christmas* クリスマス

Non-profit Organization for AIDS Relief／
AIDS救済非営利団体
USA 1994
CL: Under One Roof
CD, AD, D: Mark Sackett
D: Wayne Sakamoto / James Sakamoto
I: David Diaz
DF: Sackett Design Associates

1

1 *Christmas* クリスマス

Non-profit Organization for AIDS Relief／
AIDS救済非営利団体
USA 1994
CL: Under One Roof
CD, AD, D: Mark Sackett
D: Wayne Sakamoto / James Sakamoto
I: David Diaz
DF: Sackett Design Associates

2

2 *Christmas* クリスマス

Design Firm／デザイン
Taiwan 1997
CL, DF: Leslie Chan Design Co., Ltd.
CD, AD, D: Leslie Chan Wing Kei
D, I: Huang Yi Tang

Christmas クリスマス

Graphic Design Consultancy／
グラフィックデザインコンサルタント
Singapore 1995
CL, DF: Design Objectives Pte Ltd.
CD, AD, D: Ronnie Tan

Christmas クリスマス

Museum／美術館
USA 1996
CL: Museum of Modern Art
CD: Stefan Sagmeister
D, I: Susanne Poelleriteer
DF: Sagmeister Inc.

1 *Christmas* クリスマス

Photo Studio／フォトスタジオ
Singapore 1994
CL: KF Seetoh Photography
CD, AD, D: Ronnie Tan
DF: Design Objectives Pte Ltd.

2 *Christmas* クリスマス

Architects／建築設計
Australia 1995
CL: The Buchan Group
CD, D: Karel Wöhlnick
DF: Wöhlnick Design

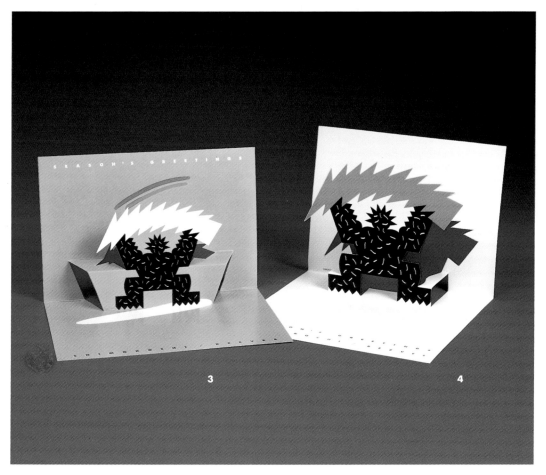

3,4 *Seasonal Greeting*
季節のあいさつ状

Design Consultants／デザインコンサルタント
USA 1995 (4) / 1996 (3)
CL, DF: Shimokochi / Reeves
CD, AD, D: Mamoru Shimokochi
AD: Anne Reeves

Christmas　クリスマス

Film Production／映像プロダクション
Germany 1996
CL: HKF Film-und Fernseh Produktion
D, I: Uwe Melichar
CW: Hannah S. Fricke
DF: Factor Design

Christmas　クリスマス

Design Firm／デザイン
USA 1996
CL, DF: Greteman Group
CD, AD, D: Sonia Greteman
AD, D: James Strange

Christmas クリスマス

Design Consultants／デザインコンサルタント
Australia 1995
CL, DF: Sophie Bartho & Associates
CD, AD, D: Sophie Bartho
I: Barry Olive

New Year 年賀状

Design Consultants／デザインコンサルタント
Australia 1996
CL, DF: Sophie Bartho & Associates
CD, AD, D: Sophie Bartho

袋の中には塩、胡椒、スパイス、シーズニングが入っている。
調味料（シーズニング）とシーズン・グリーティングをかけている。
The bag contains salt, pepper, spices, and seasonings.
A pun using the words "Seasonings" and "Season's Greetings."

Christmas クリスマス

Design Firm／デザイン
Germany 1995
CL, DF: Factor Design
D: Olaf Stein

Christmas クリスマス

Architects／建築設計
Australia 1996
CL: The Buchan Group
CD, D: Karel Wöhlnick
DF: Wöhlnick Design

1

2

3

1 *Christmas*　クリスマス

Gift & Stationery Supplier
／ギフト商品、グリーティングカードの企画・販売
Japan　1996
CL: ㈱サンリオ　Sanrio Co., Ltd.

カードに付いているスイッチを押すとクリスマスソングが流れる。
Push the button on the front of the card to play a Christmas song.

2,3 *Christmas*　クリスマス

Stationery Supplier／カード、アートグッズ企画販売
Japan　1996
CL: ギャラリービー・ビー・イー　gallery B. B. E.
D: 小林 智香枝　Chikae Kobayashi (2) ／
永末優子　Yuko Nagasue (3)

1,2 Christmas クリスマス

Design Firm／デザイン
Malaysia 1992 (1) / 1994 (2)
CL, DF: Punctuation Creative Co.
CD, AD, D: Ping
CD, AD: Vincent Pang (1)
CW: Ping (2)
I: Alex (2)
Scrap Art: Gan (1)

Christmas クリスマス

Food Manufacturer／食品
Hong Kong 1996
CL: Lee Kum Kee Co., Ltd.
CD, AD, D, CW: Grand So
AD, D: Rex Lee
D: Ringo Lam
CW: Johnson Cheng
Production Manager: Raymond Au
DF: Grand Design Company

Seasonal Greeting
季節のあいさつ状

Design Firm, Paper Supplier／
デザイン, 製紙販売
Malaysia 1995
CL: Punctutation Creative Co. / Hiap Mott
CD, AD, D: Ping
I: Alex
DF: Punctuation Creative Co.

1

2

3

1 *Christmas* クリスマス

Stationery Supplier／ステーショナリーメーカー
Japan 1996
CL: ㈱イソップ Æsop Co., Ltd.
D, I: 畑澤克年 Katsutoshi Hatazawa

2 *Christmas* クリスマス

Gift & Stationery Supplier
／ギフト商品、グリーティングカードの企画・販売
Japan 1996
CL: ㈱サンリオ Sanrio Co., Ltd.

カードに付いているスイッチを押すとクリスマスソングが流れる。
Push the button on the front of the card to play a Christmas song.

3 *Christmas* クリスマス

Stationery Supplier／カード、アートグッズ企画販売
Japan 1996
CL: グラフィックステーション graphic station
D: 菊池典子 Noriko Kikuchi

1,2 *Christmas* クリスマス

Apparel Maker／アパレルメーカー
Japan 1995 (2) / 1996 (1)
CL: ポール・スミス・ジャパン Paul Smith Japan
AD: Alan Aboud

Christmas クリスマス

Personal／個人
France 1996
CL, CD, AD, D, I: Frédéric Bortolotti

Christmas クリスマス

Design Firm／デザイン
USA 1993
CL, DF: Sackett Design Associates
CD, AD, D: Mark Sackett
D: Wayne Sakamoto /
 James Sakamoto
I: Michael Loggins /
 Heidi Streeter

Christmas クリスマス

Museum／美術館
USA 1995
CL: Museum of Modern Art
CD, AD: Cara Orr
D, I: Steven Guarnaccia
CW: Museum of Modern Art

1 *Christmas* クリスマス

Design Firm／デザイン
UK 1991
CL, DF: Holmes Knight Ritchie TBWA
CD: David Holmes
AD, D, CW: Murray Partridge
I: Dovrat Ben-Nahum
Illustrator's Agent in Japan: CWC

2 *Christmas* クリスマス

Auto Manufacturer／自動車メーカー
Japan 1992
CL: トヨタ Toyota
CD: 天野 知恵美 Chiemi Amano
AD: 戸田幸治 Koji Toda
CW: こしみず幸三 Kozo Koshimizu

3,4 *Christmas* クリスマス

Greeting Card Company／カード製造販売
USA 1996
CL: Nobleworks
CD, CW: Christopher Noble
AD: Connie Scharar
I: Steven Guarnaccia

Christmas クリスマス

Design Firm／デザイン
USA 1993
CL ,DF: Rickabaugh Graphics
AD: Eric Rickabaugh
D, CW: Mark Krumel

Christmas クリスマス

Film Production／映像プロダクション
Australia 1996
CL: Great Southern Films
AD, D: Andrew Hoyne
P: Peter Rosetzky
DF: Andrew Hoyne Design

Christmas クリスマス

Design Firm／デザイン
USA 1992
CL, CW, DF: White Plus
CD: Ken White
AD: Trina Nuovo

Christmas クリスマス

Non-profit Organization／非営利団体
USA 1992
CL: Amateur Athletic Foundation of
Los Angeles
CD: Ken White
AD: Trina Nuovo
DF: White Plus

Christmas クリスマス

Advertising Agency／広告代理店
UK 1992
CL: WH Smith Group
CD: Iain Crockart
D: Laura Heard
I: Dovrat Ben-Nahum
DF: Cat Design
Illustrator's Agent in Japan: CWC

Christmas クリスマス

Museum／美術館
UK 1991
CL, DF: Royal Academy of Art
AD: Venessa Ramm
D: Diane Talbot
I, CW: Dovrat Ben-Nahum
Illustrator's Agent in Japan: CWC

Christmas クリスマス

Design Firm／デザイン
France 1996
CL: Cozzolinoellett
I: Jeff Fisher
Illustrator's Agent in Japan: CWC

Christmas クリスマス

Computer Consultant／コンピュータコンサルタント
Australia 1996
CL: Mark Linton Smith
AD, D: Andrew Hoyne
D: Anna Svigos
I: Angela Ho
DF: Andrew Hoyne Design

Christmas クリスマス

Illustrator／イラストレーター
France 1994
CL, D, I: Serge Clerc

1,2 *Christmas* クリスマス

Telecommunications／テレコミュニケーション
USA 1995 (2) / 1996 (1)
CL: Brite Voice Systems
CD, AD, D: Sonia Greteman
AD, D, I: James Strange

1

2

SEASON'S GREETINGS FROHES FEST MEILLEURS VOEUX FELIZ NAVIDAD BUONE FESTE

PEACE PAIX PAZ FRIEDE PACE PEACE PAIX PAZ FRIEDE PACE PEACE PAIX PAZ FRIEDE

WARMEST

X'MAS WISHES

THE HONG KONG AND CHINA GAS COMPANY LIMITED

SEASON'S GREETINGS
ZIELANSKIs

Seasonal Greeting
季節のあいさつ状

Personal／個人
USA 1993
CL: Trudy and John Zielanski
AD, D, I: Trudy Cole-Zielanski
DF: Trudy Cole-Zielanski Design

Christmas クリスマス

Utilities／公共事業
Hong Kong 1995
CL: The Hong Kong and China Gas Co., Ltd.
CD: Kan Tai-keung
AD: Eddy Yu Chi Kong
D: Pamela Law Pui Hang
DF: Kan & Lau Design Consultants

Christmas クリスマス

Film Production／映像プロダクション
Germany 1995
CL: HKF Film-und Fernseh Produktion
D, I: Rüdiger Goetz
DF: Factor Design

P.140 Seasonal Greeting
季節のあいさつ状

Greeting Card Company／カード製造販売
USA 1996
CL: Elizabeth Charles, Inc.
CD, D: Tom Jenkins / Jane Jenkins
DF: The Design Foundry

White-footed Lemur

Chester White Boar

White-nosed Monkey

Christmas クリスマス

Personal／個人
USA 1994
CL: Trudy and John Zielanski
AD, D, I: Trudy Cole-Zielanski
DF: Trudy Cole-Zielanski Design

聖夜(holy night)と沢山穴の開いた(holey)騎士(knight)とかけている。
A play on words using "Holy Night" and "holey knight."

White-tailed Deer

White-lipped Peccary

Christmas クリスマス

Design Firm／デザイン
USA 1993
CL, CW, DF: White Plus
CD: Ken White
AD: Trina Nuovo

Christmas クリスマス

Design Firm／デザイン
USA 1994
CL, DF: White Plus
CD, CW: Ken White
AD, CW: Trina Nuovo
P: Sherry Etheredge

Christmas　クリスマス

Graphic Designer／グラフィックデザイナー
USA 1993
CL, AD, D, CW: Jennifer Kennard
DF: Arti Factory

Christmas　クリスマス

Graphic Designer／グラフィックデザイナー
USA 1996
CL, AD, D, I, CW: Jennifer Kennard
DF: The Ravenna Press

Christmas クリスマス

Design Firm／デザイン
USA 1995
CL, DF: Sackett Design Associates
CD, AD, D: Mark Sackett
D: Wayne Sakamoto / James Sakamoto

Christmas クリスマス

Architecture／建築、設計
Germany 1994
CL: BKB Architekten
D: Jan Wohlenberg
DF: Vierviertel Gestaltung

Christmas クリスマス

Visual Communication Design／デザイン
Canada 1993
CL, DF: Zacharko Design Partnership
CD, D, CW: Theresa Zacharko
D: Terrance Zacharko

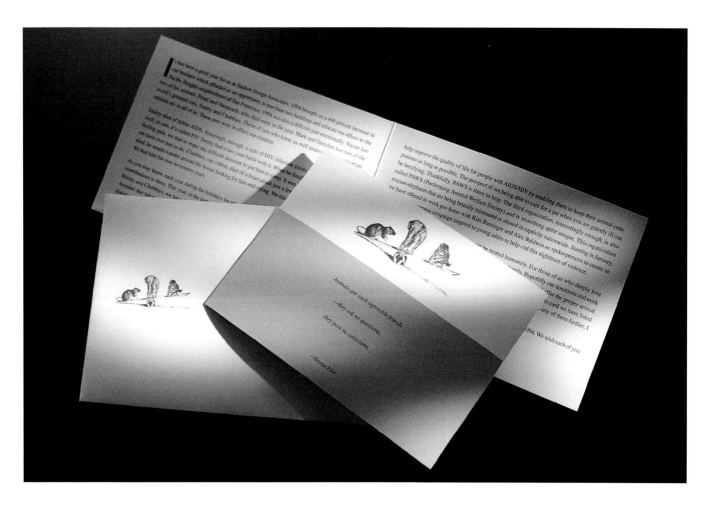

Christmas クリスマス

Design Firm／デザイン
USA 1994
CL, DF: Sackett Design Associates
CD, AD, D: Mark Sackett
D: Wayne Sakamoto / James Sakamoto

P.146 *Christmas*
クリスマス

Design Firm／デザイン
Yugoslavia 1996
CL, CD, AD, D, CW, DF: Škart Group

Christmas クリスマス

Design Consultants／デザインコンサルタント
Australia 1995
CL ,DF: Spatchurst Design
CD, AD, D, I: Steven Joseph

Christmas クリスマス

Design Firm／デザイン
Yugoslavia 1995
CL, DF: Trans:East
CD, AD: Jovan Jelovac
AD, D: Srdan Apostolović

Christmas クリスマス

Design Firm／デザイン
Australia 1996
CL, DF: Wöhlnick Design
CD, D: Karel Wöhlnick
D: Damien West
I: Jude Hendrix

A collection of things to help you spread the festive message

We would like to wish you a joyous festive season and a bright and colourful New year.

A collection of things to help you spread the festive message

Simply cut out the individual panels and place it on windows, walls, ceilings etc. and colour in with snow paint.

Christmas クリスマス

Landscape Architects／ランドスケープ
Australia 1996
CL: Plan (E)
CD, AD, D: Karel Wöhlnick
D: Damien West
P: James Rogers
DF: Wöhlnick Design

CREATIVE SPIRIT

TRANSFORMED

Christmas クリスマス

Design Consultants／デザインコンサルタント
Australia 1995
CL, DF: Spatchurst Design
CD, AD, D: John Spatchurst

Christmas クリスマス

Advertising Agency／広告企画制作
Germany 1995
CL: Springer & Jacobi
D: Johannes Erler
DF: Factor Design

New Year 年賀状

Design Firm／デザイン
USA 1995
CL, DF: Matsumoto, Inc.
CD, AD, D: Takaaki Matsumoto

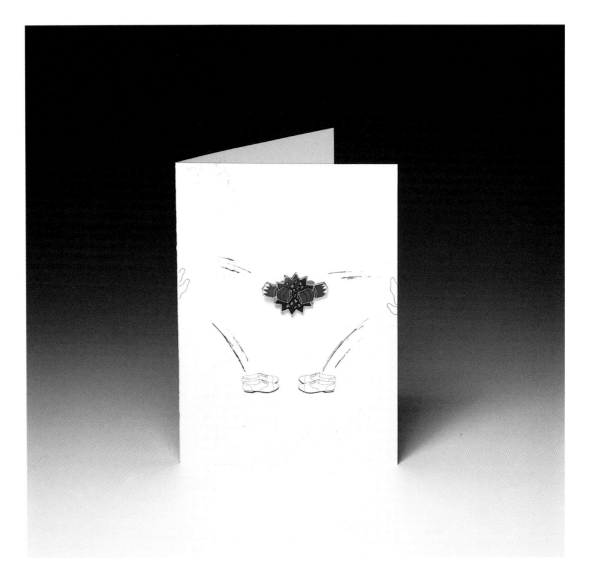

Christmas クリスマス

Designers／デザイナー
UK 1989
CL, DF: Trickett & Webb Ltd.
CD, D: Brian Webb / Lynn Trickett
D: Andy Thomas

Christmas クリスマス

Paper Manufacturer／製紙
Australia 1995
CL: Australian Paper
CD, AD, D, I: David Lancashire
DF: David Lancashire Design

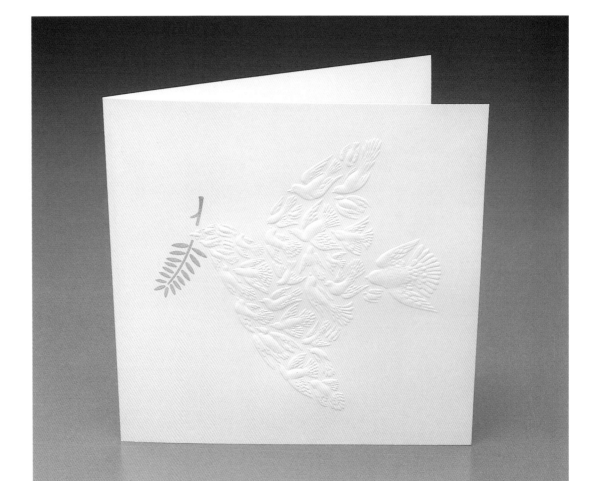

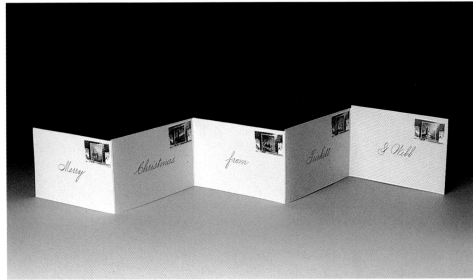

Christmas クリスマス

Designers／デザイナー
UK 1990
CL, DF: Trickett & Webb Ltd.
CD, D: Brian Webb / Lynn Trickett
D, I: Andy Thomas

Christmas クリスマス

Metalworking Machines Factory／機械製造所
Portugal 1995
CL: Guifil
AD, D: Emanuel Barbosa
DF: Emanuel Barbosa Design

1.2 *Christmas* クリスマス

Design Firm／デザイン
Italy 1996 (2) / 1997 (1)
CL, DF: AREA-Strategic Design
GD, CW: Antonio Romano
D: Stefania Cinquini
P: Giuseppe Maria Fadda
I: Francesca Montosi / Anna Fetel (1)

Christmas クリスマス

Design Firm／デザイン
Italy 1996
CL, DF: AREA-Strategic Design
CD, CW: Antonio Romano
D: Fabio Finocchioli
P: Giuseppe Maria Fadda
I: Anna Fetel

Christmas クリスマス

Food Manufacturer／食品
Italy 1996
CL: Cirio
CD: Antonio Romano
D: Stefania Cinquini
P: Giuseppe Maria Fadda
I: Anna Fetel
DF: AREA-Strategic Design

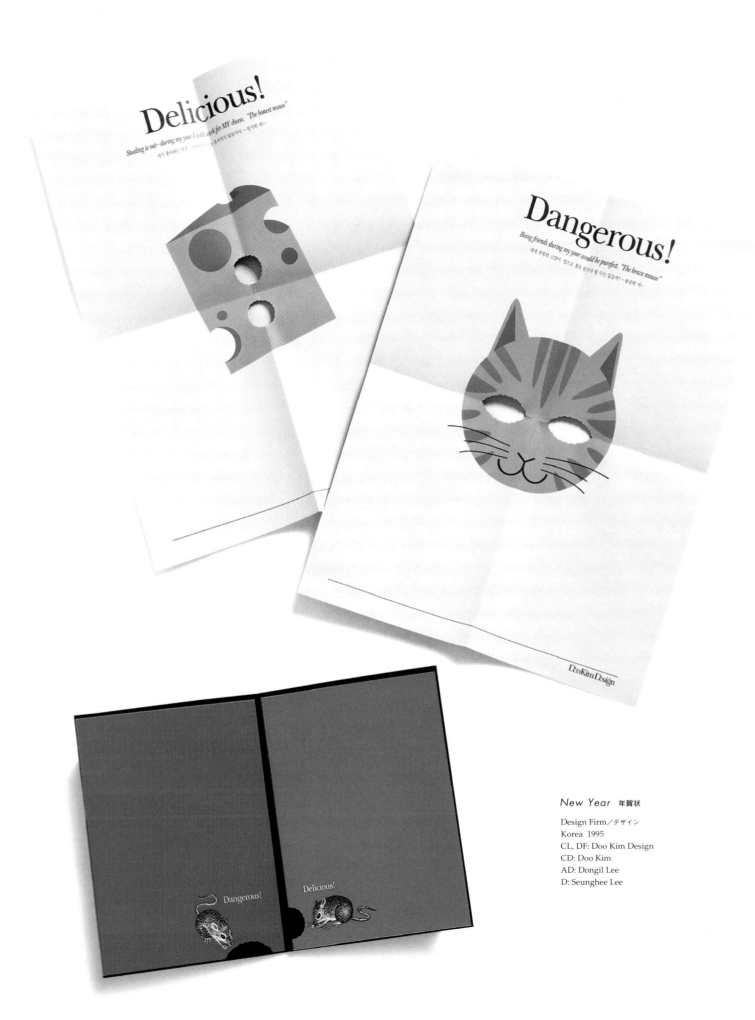

Delicious!

Stealing is out--during my year I will work for MY cheese. "The honest mouse"

Dangerous!

Being friends during my year would be purrfect. "The brave mouse"

DooKim Design

Dangerous!   Delicious!

New Year 年賀状

Design Firm／デザイン
Korea 1995
CL, DF: Doo Kim Design
CD: Doo Kim
AD: Dongil Lee
D: Seunghee Lee

Christmas クリスマス

Design Firm／デザイン
USA 1995
CL, DF: Rickabaugh Graphics
CD, AD, D, I, CW: Eric Rickabaugh

New Year 年賀状

Design Firm／デザイン
Denmark 1994
CL, DF: Gyllan Grafixx
CD, AD, D: Peter Gyllan

"white plus•••"

Christmas クリスマス

Design Firm／デザイン
USA 1996
CL, DF: White Plus
CD: Trina Nuovo
D: Jiyoon Jun
P: Benson Ng
CW: Daryl Forkell

New Year 年賀状

Design Firm／デザイン
Japan 1997
CL, DF: ㈱パッケージング クリエイト
Packaging Create Inc.
AD, D: 奥村昭夫　Akio Okumura

Chinese New Year
年賀状

Design Firm／デザイン
France 1997
CL: evansandwong
CD: Christoper Evans / Victor Wong

P.159 *New Year* 年賀状

Design Firm／デザイン
USA 1993
CL, DF: The Johnson Studios
CD, D, CW: Heidi Johnson

New Year 年賀状

Graphic Design & Advertising／
グラフィックデザイン＆広告
USA 1993
CL, DF: Dyer / Mutchnick Group Inc.
CD, AD, D: Rod Dyer

THE JOHNSON STUDIOS
MAHMOOD FARUQI
C/O ARROWSTREET
ELM STREET
SOMERVILLE, MA
FIVE HOLLIS PARK CAMBRIDGE, MA
PAR AVION
AERPHOST
JULY
FOUR SEASONS
BOOK OF MONTHS 1994
THE JOHNSON STUDIOS
FIVE HOLLIS PARK CAMBRIDGE, MA 02140

New Year 年賀状

Architecture & Package Design／
建築設計＆パッケージデザイン
Japan 1996
CL: プラン・Y Plan・Y
CD, AD, D: 吉田美幸 Miyuki Yoshida

New Year 年賀状

Design Firm／デザイン
Japan 1993
CL, DF: ㈱パッケージング クリエイト
Packaging Create Inc.
AD, D: 奥村昭夫　Akio Okumura

New Year 年賀状

Design Firm／デザイン
Japan 1994
CL., DF: ㈱パッケージング クリエイト
Packaging Create Inc.
AD, D: 奥村昭夫　Akio Okumura

New Year 年賀状

Architecture & Package Design／
建築設計＆パッケージデザイン
Japan 1995
CL: プラン・Y Plan・Y
CD, AD, D: 吉田美幸 Miyuki Yoshida

FELICES OPORTUNIDADES

ORIGAMI: MARCOS

TENGAMOS LISTAS
LAS ANTENAS
Y PREPAREMONOS
PARA EL GRAN SALTO.

VICTOR GARCIA / ADRIANA ELLINGER
DISEÑO Y COMUNICACION VISUAL

New Year 年賀状

Design Firm／デザイン
Argentina 1991
CL: Victor Garcia
CD, AD, D, I, CW: Victor Garcia
I, Origami: Marcos Garcia
DF: Victor Garcia & Adriana Ellinger

New Year　年賀状

Design Firm／デザイン
Hong Kong 1996
CL, DF: Grand Design Company
CD, D: Grand So
AD, D, I: Rex Lee
D, P: Ringo Lam
D: Chu Ching / Raymond Au / Candy Chan
Production Manager: Raymond Au

Chinese New Year
年賀状

Design Firm／デザイン
Malaysia 1994
CL, DF: Punctuation Creative Co.
CD, AD, D, CW: Ping
I: Alex

Chinese New Year
年賀状

Design Firm／デザイン
Malaysia 1996
CL, DF: Punctuation Creative Co.
CD, AD, D: Ping
I: Alex

切り離すと短冊になり、旧正月の飾り付けに使える。
Cut into strips to make a Chinese New Year decoration.

1 Chinese New Year
年賀状

Design Firm／デザイン
Malaysia 1993
CL, DF: Punctuation Creative Co.
CD, AD, D: Vincent Pang / Ping

2 New Year 年賀状

Designer／デザイナー
Singapore 1997
CL, CD, AD, D, I: Hon Soo Tien

1

2

New Year 年賀状

Design Firm／デザイン
Hong Kong 1996
CL, DF: Kan & Lau Design Consultants
CD, AD, D: Kan Tai-keung
AD, D: Freeman Lau Siu Hong / Eddy Yu Chi Kong
D: Benson Kwun Tin Yau / Joyce Ho Ngai Sing /
Veronica Cheung Lai Sheung / James Leung Wai Mo /
Man Lee Che Man / Pamela Paw Pui Hang /
Patrick Fung Kai Bong

New Year 年賀状

Design Firm／デザイン   Hong Kong 1997
CL, DF: Kan & Lau Design Consultants   CD, D: Kan Tai-keung
AD, D: Freeman Lau Siu Hong / Chau So Hing
D: Eddy Yu Chi Kong / Benson Kwun Tin Yau / Veronica Cheung Lai Sheung /
Fanny Ng Wai Han / Leung Wai Yin / Joseph Leung Chun Wai / Lam Wai Hung / Stephen Lau Yu Cheong

New Year　年賀状

Apparel Maker／アパレルメーカー
Italy 1995
CL: Benetton
CD: Oliviero Toscani
D: Tibor Kalman
P: From COLORS Magazines

New Year　年賀状

Graphic Designer／グラフィックデザイナー
USA 1997
CL, DF: Susanne Schropp Design
CD, AD, D: Susanne Schropp
P: Andi Hechenberger
CW: Dayna Davis

占いのおまけが付いている。
A fortune-telling oracle is enclosed.

New Year　年賀状

Graphic Designer／グラフィックデザイナー
Mexico 1995
CL, CD, AD, D, DF: Patrick Burgeff

New Year　年賀状

Personal／個人
Germany 1995
CL, D, I: Uwe Melichar

169

New Year 年賀状

Design Firm／デザイン
Korea 1996
CL, DF: Doo Kim Design
CD: Doo Kim
AD: Dongil Lee
D: Vincent Cho
P: With Studio
CW: Scott Kim

The OX is always willing to help a friend.

OX
COLLECTION

牛 年出生的人積極進取，有堅定信心，
遇到困難時會流露出不屈不撓的堅強意志；
且為人寬厚，品性善良，是眾人心目中的知己良伴。

Enterprising and diligent, those born in the
Year of the Ox always show strong
determination in the face of difficulties.
Appreciated for its reliable character,
the Ox is cherished among friends for
its honesty and good-natured
temperament.

New Year 年賀状

Photographic Service／フォトサービス
Hong Kong 1996
CL: AGFA Hong Kong Ltd.
CD, AD: Steve Lau
D, I: Henry Lau
CW: Lee Wolter Co., Ltd.
DF: Twice Graphics

1

1 9 9 7

Zoek de juiste stukjes bij elkaar en stel uw persoonlijke kerstbonus samen.

Met onze dank voor de prettige relatie gedurende het afgelopen jaar, wensen wij u plezierige feestdagen en een gezond en succesvol 1997.

kerstpuzzel Grafisch Papier

This is your lucky X-mas

happy newyear
A PRODUCTION

4

1995

2

3

TRUUS HUIBERS
CHANTAL V/D SLUIS

1
9
9
6

AGENT-X
WISHES YOU LOTS OF LUCK AND A
HAPPY NEWYEAR
NEW ADRESS:

1,4 New Year 年賀状

Paper Manufacturer／製紙 (1)
Photographers' Agent／写真家エージェント (4)
Netherlands 1995 (4) / 1996 (1)
CL: Grafisch Papier (1) / Agent-X (4)
CD: Truus Huijbers (4)
AD, D: Petra Janssen / Edwin Vollebergh
I, DF: Studio Boot

2,3 New Year 年賀状

Graphic Designer／グラフィックデザイナー
Japan 1993 (3) / 1994 (2)
CL, AD, D: 金子正剛 Seigo Kaneko

171

New Year 年賀状

Design Firm／デザイン
UK 1992
CL, DF: Form
CD, AD, D: Paula Benson / Paul West

New Year 年賀状

Design Firm／デザイン
UK 1993
CL, DF: Form
CD, AD, D: Paul West / Paula Benson
D: Lisa Smith

New Year 年賀状

Creative Services Agency／クリエイティブサービス
USA 1992
CL: Pen Plus Inc.
CD, AD, D: Takaaki Matsumoto
DF: Matsumoto, Inc.

1,2 *New Year* 年賀状 (1)
Christmas クリスマス (2)

Apparel Maker／アパレルメーカー
Japan 1994
CL: バルーインク Barreaux Inc.
CD, AD: 淺埜 勝 Katsu Asano
D: 米澤帛笑 Kinue Yonezawa
DF: ㈱アーサー・ハンドレッド・カンパニー
ASA 100 Company

New Year 年賀状

Designer／デザイナー
Japan 1985
CL, AD: 勝井三雄 Mitsuo Katsui

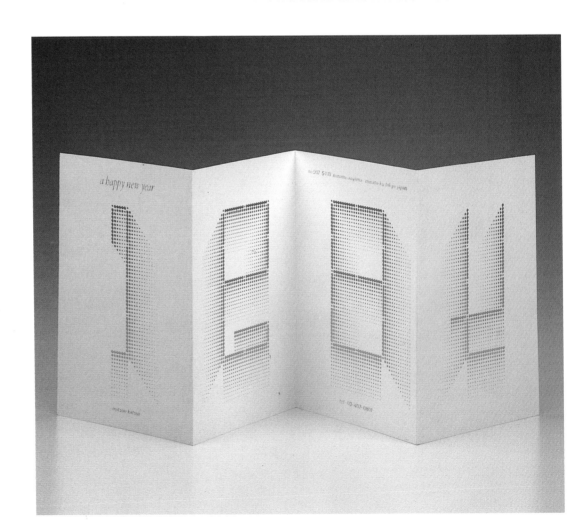

New Year 年賀状

Designer／デザイナー
Japan 1984
CL, AD: 勝井三雄 Mitsuo Katsui

New Year 年賀状

Real Estate Agent／不動産
Netherlands 1996
CL: Wijnstra Makelaardij BV
CD, AD, D: Wout de Vringer
DF: Faydherbe / de Vringer

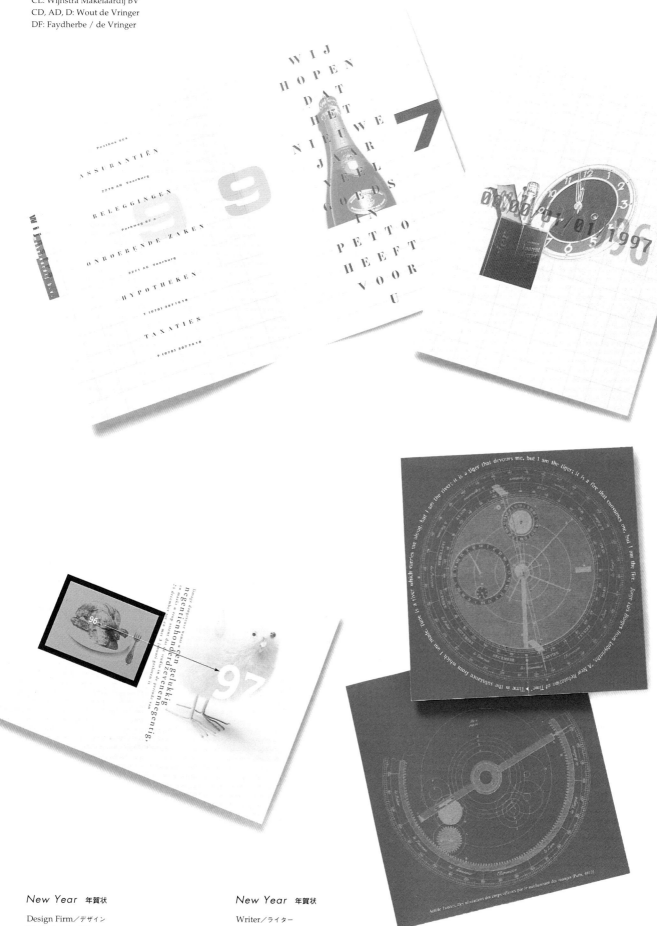

New Year 年賀状

Design Firm／デザイン
Netherlands 1996
CL, CD, AD, D: Limage Dangereuse
P: Hans de Jong

New Year 年賀状

Writer／ライター
USA 1995
CL, CW: Phil Landa
CD, AD, D: Jane Cuthbertson
DF: Myriad Inc.

New Year 年賀状

Design Firm／デザイン
USA 1994
CL: Sheaff Dorman Purins
CD, AD, D, CW: Uldis Purins

New Year 年賀状

Design Firm／デザイン
Denmark 1997
CL, DF: Gyllan Grafixx
CD, AD, D: Peter Gyllan

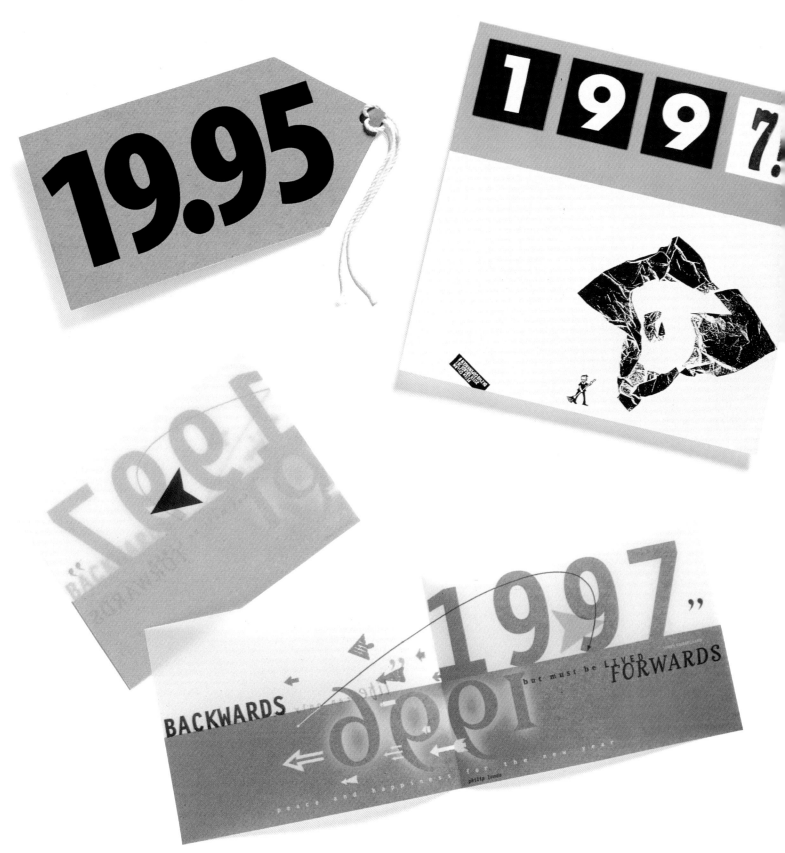

New Year 年賀状

Writer／ライター
USA 1996
CL: Phil Landa
CD, AD: Jane Cuthbertson
D: Kristy Jennings
DF: Myriad Inc.

New Year 年賀状

Advertising Agency／広告企画制作
Thailand 1995
CL, DF: Wunderman Thailand
CD, CW: Catherine Howley
AD: Jagrit Suebsanguan
D: Linda Theerakulchai

New Year 年賀状

Design Firm／デザイン
Hong Kong 1996
CL, DF: Teamwork Design Ltd.
CD, AD, D, I: Gary Tam
D, I: Joey Ong

New Year 年賀状

Design Firm／デザイン
Japan 1993
CL, D, DF: ミュゼ Musée
AD, P: 福田隆志 Takashi Fukuda

New Year　年賀状

Design Firm／デザイン
Fashion Importer & Retailer／
インポートファッション販売
Japan 1997
CL: ㈱アルトカンポ ALTO CAMPO COMPANY
AD: 高畑 小百合 Sayuri Takahata
D: 高畑三穂 Miho Takahata ／
松井 薫 Kaoru Matsui ／ 久保憲子 Noriko Kubo ／
外崎和子 Kazuko Tonosaki ／
木村智子 Tomoko Kimura ／ 韓 寿江 Sugang Kan

New Year　年賀状

Design Firm／デザイン
Argentina 1990
CL: Victor Garcia
CD, AD, D, CW: Victor Garcia
DF: Victor Garcia & Adriana Ellinger

MCMXCIはローマ数字で1991を意味している。
"MCMXCI" is "1991" in Roman numerals.

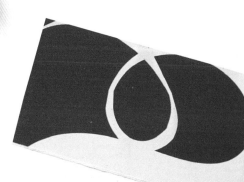

New Year　年賀状

Printing Firm／印刷
Slovenia 1996
CL: GRAF
CD, AD, CW: Eduard Cehovin

New Year　年賀状

Graphic Designer／グラフィックデザイナー
Mexico 1994
CL, CD, AD, D, DF: Patrick Burgeff

New Year 年賀状

Design Firm／デザイン
Japan 1996
CL, DF: アール・ビー・エム・デザインスタジオ
r. p. m. Design Studio
CD, AD: 高橋洋一 Yoichi Takahashi
D: 高橋敏子 Toshiko Takahashi

あけましておめでとうございます。
こんなに近くなりました。今年もよろしくお願いします。

平成九年元旦 吉野修平

一年中良い日で平和でありますように。

1,2 *New Year* 年賀状

Design Firm／デザイン
Japan 1995 (2) / 1996 (1)
CL: ㈲ヨシノデザインオフィス Yoshino Design Office
AD, D: 吉野修平 Shuhei Yoshino

New Year 年賀状

Designer／デザイナー
Singapore 1996
CL: Hon Soo Tien
CD, AD, D, I: Hon Soo Tien

New Year 年賀状

Package Design & Planning／パッケージデザイン&企画
Japan 1997
CL: ㈱パッケージランド Package Land Co., Ltd.
CD, AD, D: 田中康夫 Yasuo Tanaka

1

2

3

1,3 *New Year* 年賀状

Design Firm／デザイン
Japan 1995 (3) / 1996 (1)
CL, DF: ㈱パッケージング クリエイト
Packaging Create Inc.
AD, D: 奥村昭夫 Akio Okumura

2 *New Year* 年賀状

Package Design & Planning／パッケージデザイン＆企画
Japan 1996
CL: ㈱パッケージランド Package Land Co., Ltd.
CD, AD, D: 田中康夫 Yasuo Tanaka

New Year 年賀状

Illustrator／イラストレーター
France 1995
CL, D, I: Serge Clerc

Illustrator／イラストレーター
France 1996
CL, I: Emmanuel Pierre
Illustrator's Agent in Japan: CWC

Corbasson

Illustrator／イラストレーター
France 1997
CL, I: Dominique Corbasson
Illustrator's Agent in Japan: CWC

Best wishes to all of you
for the next months.
We are almost completely settled and enjoy very
much the inundations (floods) of light and the
stupendous panorama. Not far at all from Dominique and François, we often organise Japanese suppers
and taste many new sakes.
Lots of love.
Emmanuel
&
François.

NOUVELLE ADRESSE:
18, rue Choron, 75009-Paris
Tél. Emmanuel Pierre: 40 23 06 23
Tél. François Motte: 40 23 92 86
Télécopie: 40 23 09 23

New Year 年賀状

Illustrator／イラストレーター
USA 1997
CL, I: Pamela Hobbs

New Year 年賀状

Illustrator／イラストレーター
USA 1996
CL, I: Pamela Hobbs

New Year 年賀状

Illustrator & Designer／
イラストレーター＆デザイナー
USA 1992-96
CL, CD, AD, D, I, CW, DF: Michael Bartalos

1

2

3

4

5

1,2,3,4,5 New Year　年賀状

Design Firm／デザイン
Switzerland 1991 (1) / 1992 (2) /
1993 (4) / 1994 (5) / 1995 (3)
CL, DF: AND Trafic Grafic
CD, AD, D, P: Jean-Benoît Lévy

Seasonal Greeting
季節のあいさつ状

Architects／建築
Netherlands 1994
CL: BNA Architektenburo
Roeleveld-Sikkes BV
CD, AD, D: Wout de Vringer
CW: Jan Van Huizen
DF: Faydherbe / de Vringer

1

2

1,2 New Year 年賀状

Design Firm／デザイン
USA 1995 (2) / 1996 (1)
CL: ReVerb
AD, D: Somi Kim
AD: Whitney Lowe / Lisa Nugent / Susan Parr
P (1), I (1,2): James W. Moore

New Year 年賀状

Design Firm／デザイン
France 1996
CL, DF: Sabotage! Entertainment
AD, D: Guillaume Wolf

tik. tak. tic. tac. tik. tak. tic. tac. tik. tak. tic. tac. tik. tak. tic. tac. tik. tak. tic. tac. tik. tak. tic. tac. tik. tak. tic. tac. tik. tak. tic.

Kako čas teče!

edi berk

1995

andrej mlakar

1996

good job!

KIRIMA DESIGN OFFICE

KIRIMA DESIGN OFFICE

1

2

3

4

1 *New Year* 年賀状

Designer & Architect／デザイナー＆建築家
Slovenia 1995
CL: Edi Berk / Andrej Mlakar
AD, D: Edi Berk
DF: KROG

2 *New Year* 年賀状

Stylist／スタイリスト
Japan 1997
CL: 堂下奈鼓 Nako Doshita
AD, P: 福田隆志 Takashi Fukuda
D, DF: ミュゼ Musée

3,4 *New Year* 年賀状

Design Firm／デザイン
Japan 1994 (3) / 1995 (4)
CL: キリマデザイン事務所 Kirima Design Office
AD, D: 切間晴美 Harumi Kirima
D: 湯川史隆 Fumitaka Yukawa

Seasonal Greeting
季節のあいさつ状

Design, Advertising, and Marketing Firm／
デザイン, 広告, マーケティング
USA 1995
CL, DF: Greteman Group
CD, AD, D: Sonia Greteman
AD, D: James Strange

Seasonal Greeting
季節のあいさつ状

Publisher／出版
Australia 1995
CL: Cicada Press
CD, AD, D, I: David Lancashire
DF: David Lancashire Design

Autumn Greeting
季節のあいさつ状（秋）

Architecture & Package Design／
建築設計＆パッケージデザイン
Japan 1995
CL: プラン Y Plan Y
CD, AD, D: 吉田美幸 Miyuki Yoshida

小秋銀簾淡風起

1995年9月
PLAN Y

St. Valentine's Day
バレンタインデー

Design Firm／デザイン
Fashion Importer & Retailer／
インポート／ファッション販売
Japan 1997
CL: 株アルトカンポ ALTO CAMPO COMPANY
AD: 高畑小百合 Sayuri Takahata
D: 高畑美穂 Miho Takahata／
松井薫 Kaoru Matsui／久保憲子 Noriko Kubo／
外崎和子 Kazuko Tonosaki／
木村智子 Tomoko Kimura／韓寿江 Sugang Kan

194

1

2

3

1 *Summer Greeting*
残暑見舞

Architecture & Package Design／
建築設計＆パッケージデザイン
Japan 1996
CL: プラン・Y Plan·Y
CD, AD, D: 吉田美幸 Miyuki Yoshida

2 *Seasonal Greeting*
季節のあいさつ状

Festival Organizer／フェスティバル主催
Netherlands 1994
CL: Rotterdam Festivals
CD, AD, D: Limage Dangereuse
P: Hans de Jong

3 *Summer Greeting*
暑中見舞

Design Firm／デザイン
Netherlands 1996
CL: Limage Dangereuse
CD, AD, D: Limage Dangereuse
P: Hans de Jong

Tea for 222?

LISTEN TO YOUR MOTHER!

Happy Mother's Day
from the kind of
people she
always hoped you'd
work with.

Sheaff Dorman Purins
Strategic Thinking and Design
Voice: 617.449.0602
sheaff@tiac.net
Fax: 617.455.8945
www.sheaff.com

Great design is timeless.

Mother knows best.

Want to see some real fireworks?

Then let us show you
our portfolio.

Happy Independence Day
from the independent thinkers
@ Sheaff Dorman Purins!

Sheaff Dorman Purins
Strategic Thinking and Design
Voice: 617.449.0602
sheaff@tiac.net
Fax: 617.455.8945
www.sheaff.com

BAM!

Trick or treat?

Do you believe in love at first sight?

Great.
When can we show you
our latest portfolio?

Happy Valentine's Day
from the people
you'll love to work with!

Sheaff Dorman Purins
Strategic Thinking and Design
Voice: 617.449.0602
sheaff@tiac.net
Fax: 617.455.8945

Why do they call it Labor Day?

Daylight savings begins on April 6th.

Sadie Hawkins' Day is November 1st.

But we'll accept
a design proposal
from an astute
business woman anytime.

Sheaff Dorman Purins
Strategic Thinking and Design
Voice: 781.449.0602
sheaff@tiac.net
Fax: 781.455.8945
www.sheaff.com

If Betsy Ross were alive,
we'd hire her.

Happy Flag Day
from the people
who can do a great job
using only three colors.

Sheaff Dorman Purins
Strategic Thinking and Design
Voice: 617.449.0602
sheaff@tiac.net
Fax: 617.455.8945
www.sheaff.com

Red 032 U   White U   Blue 072 U

Got a match?

1997

Seasonal Greeting
季節のあいさつ状

Design Firm／デザイン
USA 1997
CL, DF: Sheaff Dorman Purins
CD, AD, CW: Uldis Purins
D: Pat Dacey
CW: Joey Baron

New Year　年賀状

Design Firm／デザイン
Japan 1995
CL, DF: ワンストローク　One Stroke Co., Ltd.
AD, D: 駒形克己 Katsumi Komagata

1 *St. Valentine's Day*
バレンタインデー
2 *Easter*　イースター

Design Consultancy／デザインコンサルタント
UK 1997
CL: Design Narrative
CD, AD: Andy Ewan
D: Stephanie Fletcher / Vibe Bangsgaard
I: Seanaid Mackay (1)
DF: Design Narrative (2)

Seasonal Greeting
季節のあいさつ状

Food Manufacturer／食品
Australia 1996
CL: Alligator Brand
AD, D: Andrew Hoyne
I: Angela Ho
DF: Andrew Hoyne Design

Summer Greeting
暑中見舞

Design Firm／デザイン
Japan 1996
CL: 広告農場 Kokokunojyo
CD, AD, D: 紺谷宏明 Hiroaki Konya
P: HARUKI
CW: 坂内和泉 Izumi Sakauchi

Seasonal Greeting
季節のあいさつ状

Design Firm／デザイン
Hong Kong 1997
CL, DF: Teamwork Design Ltd.
CD, AD, D, I: Gary Tam
D, I: Joey Ong / Alex Chan /
Ivy Wong / Andy Lau

Seasonal Greeting
季節のあいさつ状

Shoe Company／靴製造販売
Netherlands 1996
CL: Sacha Shoes
CD: Bert Termeer
AD, D: Edwin Vollebergh / Petra Janssen
P: Agent-X Willemine Pernette
I, CW, DF: Studio Boot

Japan 1997
CL: エッチ・エー・エル HAL
CD, AD, D: 堀井敏哉 Toshiya Horii

1,3 *Spring Greeting*
季節のあいさつ状（春）
2 *St. Valentine's Day*
バレンタインデー

Design Firm／デザイン
Mexico 1996
CL: Antonio Sanchez
CD, AD, D, CW: Antonio Sanchez
DF: El Esqueleto Del Angel (+)

Summer Greeting
暑中見舞

Design Firm／デザイン
Japan 1997
CL: エッチ・エー・エル HAL
CD, AD, D: 堀井敏哉 Toshiya Horii

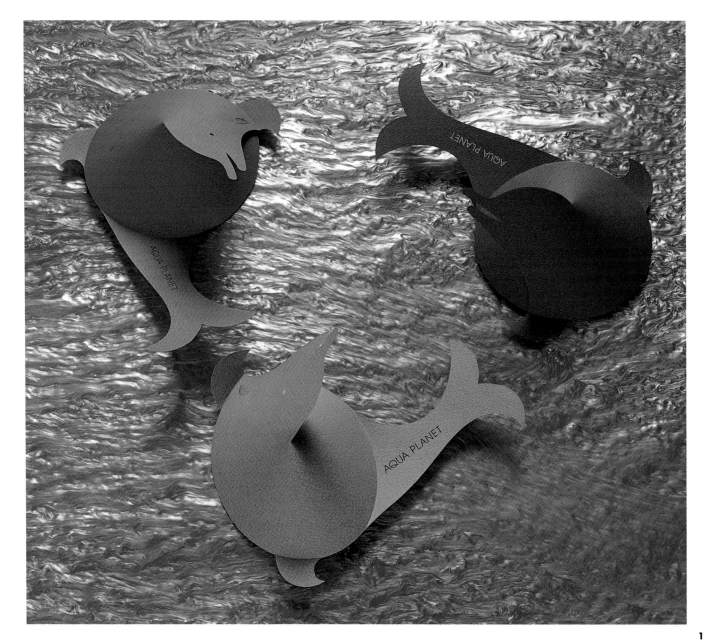

1

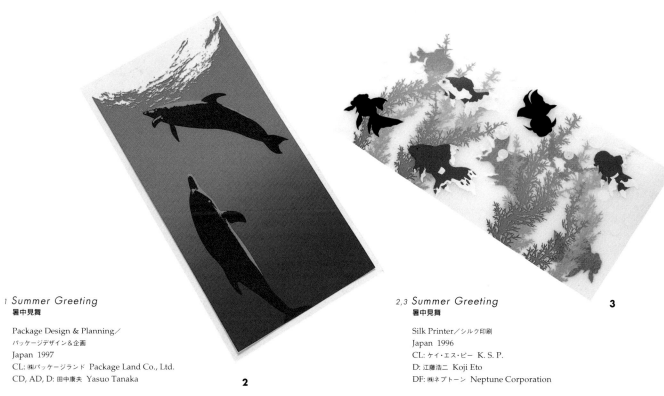

1 *Summer Greeting*
暑中見舞

Package Design & Planning／
パッケージデザイン＆企画
Japan 1997
CL: ㈱パッケージランド Package Land Co., Ltd.
CD, AD, D: 田中康夫 Yasuo Tanaka

2

2,3 *Summer Greeting*
暑中見舞

Silk Printer／シルク印刷
Japan 1996
CL: ケイ・エス・ピー K. S. P.
D: 江藤浩二 Koji Eto
DF: ㈱ネプトーン Neptune Corporation

3

1

2

3 *Seasonal Greeting*
季節のあいさつ状

Graphic Design Consultancy／
グラフィックデザインコンサルタント
Singapore 1997
CL, DF: Design Objectives Pte Ltd.
CD, AD, D: Ronnie Tan

4 *Greeting*　あいさつ状

Design Firm／デザイン
Japan 1996
CL: 原デザイン室 Hara Design Room
AD: 久住欣也 Yoshinari Hisazumi
D: 原 雄一 Yuichi Hara
DF: ヒサズミデザイン室 Hisazumi Design Room

5 *Seasonal Greeting*
季節のあいさつ状

Printer／印刷
Germany 1996
CL: Reset Grafische Medien
D: Uwe Melichar / Johannes Erler
DF: Factor Design

1,2 *Seasonal Greeting*
季節のあいさつ状

Children's Clothing Maker／子供服製造販売
Netherlands 1993
CL: Oilily
CD: Jean Philipse
AD, D, I: Edwin Vollebergh
DF: De Studio B. V.

as the season unfolds......

GREETINGS from OILILY

ずーっと
なかよしで
いましょう。

Yuichi HARA

Seasonal Greeting 季節のあいさつ状
Designer／デザイナー　Switzerland 1997　CL: Lucia Frey　CD, AD, D, I, CW: Lucia Frey　DF: Wild & Frey, Agentur für Design

others

Birthday 誕生日

Greeting Card Company／カード製造販売
USA 1996
CL: Silverdog
AD, D, I: Vittorio Costarella
DF: Modern Dog

Birthday 誕生日

Greeting Card Company／カード製造販売
USA 1996
CL: Silverdog
AD, DF: Modern Dog
D, I, CW: Michael Strassburger / Robynne Raye /
Vittorio Costarella / George Estrada /
Coby Shultz

Multi-Purpose
多目的カード

Stationery Supplier／カード・ステーショナリー企画販売
Hong Kong 1992
CL: Elegant Greetings
D: Colin Tillyer
DF: Graphicat Ltd.

Multi-Purpose
多目的カード

Design Firm／デザイン
Germany 1994
CL, CW, DF: Cyan
D: Daniela Haufe / Sophie Alex / Detlef Fiedler

Multi-Purpose
多目的カード

Museum／美術館
Mexico 1995
CL: Museo Del Calzado
CD: Carmen Artigas
AD, D, P: Antonio Sanchez
P: Gabriel Batiz / Roberto Portillo

1 *Greeting*
あいさつ状

Design Firm／デザイン
Japan 1994
CL, DF: デザイン エア design AIR
D, P: 福田明美 Akemi Fukuta

2 *Greeting*
あいさつ状

Design Firm／デザイン
Japan 1992
CL, AD, D, DF: ミュゼ Musée

3 *Greeting*
あいさつ状

Design Firm／デザイン
Japan 1996
CL, DF: ヒサズミデザイン室 Hisazumi Design Room
AD, I: 久住欣也 Yoshinari Hisazumi
P: 武田カズエ Kazue Takeda

Multi-Purpose
多目的カード

Design Firm／デザイン
USA 1996
CL, DF: Purgatory Pie Press
CD: Ester Smith
AD: Dikko Faust
I: Pamela Hobbs

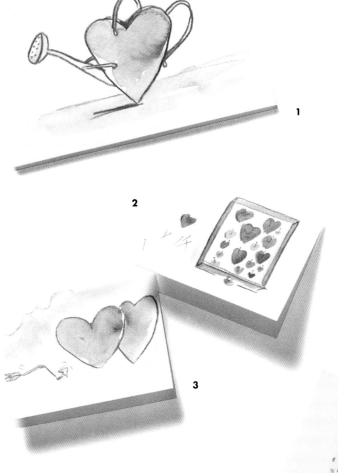

1

2

3

4

1,2,3,4 *Multi-Purpose*
多目的カード

Stationery Supplier／カード企画販売
Japan 1996
CL: ギャラリーインターフォーム
Gallery Interform
I: David Holmes (1,2,3) /
Dovrat Ben-Nahum (4)
Producer: クロスワールドコネクションズ
Cross World Connections (CWC)

Get Well Soon
御見舞

Greeting Card Company／カード製造販売
USA 1993
CL: Marcel Schurman Company
I: Steven Guarnaccia

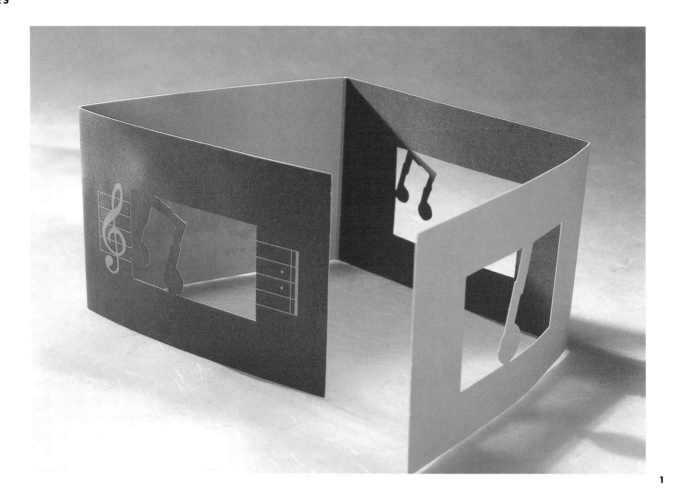

1

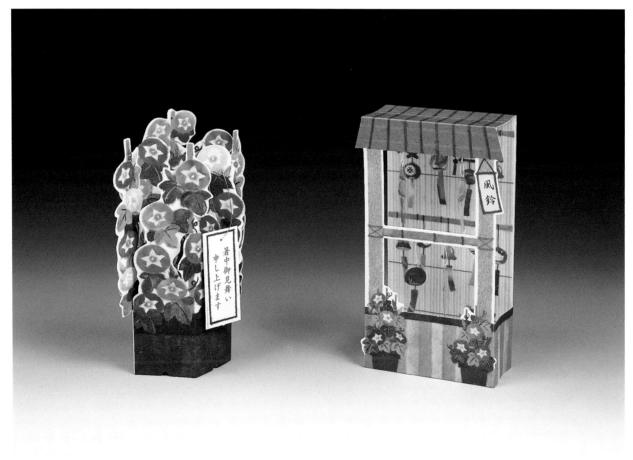

2

1 With Compliments
あいさつ状

Liquor Distributor／酒類販売
Australia 1996
CL: Swift & Moore P/L
CD: Sophie Bartho
D: Naaz Kerr
DF: Sophie Bartho & Associates

2 Greeting あいさつ状

Gift & Stationery Supplier／
ギフト商品、グリーティングカードの企画・販売
Japan 1997
CL: ㈱サンリオ Sanrio Co., Ltd.

Thank You Card 礼状

Architecture & Package Design/
建築設計＆パッケージデザイン
Japan 1995
CL: プラン・Y Plan Y
CD, AD, D: 吉田美幸 Miyuki Yoshida

THANK YOU

DECEMBER
1995

Multi-Purpose
多目的カード

Stationery Supplier/ステーショナリーメーカー
Japan 1995
CL: 油イソップ Aesop Co., Ltd
D, I: 畑澤克利 Katsutoshi Hatazawa

Birthday 誕生日

Porcelain Manufacturer／磁器製品製造販売
Germany 1996
CL: Porzellanfabrik Arzberg
CD, AD: Michael Sieger (Package)
D: Seymour Chwast (Candle Holder)
DF: Sieger Design Architektur & Design

Index of submittors

Private Greeting Cards

Designer
Yutaka Ichimura

Editor
Maya Kishida

Photographer
Kuniharu Fujimoto

English Translator
Douglas Allsopp

Typesetter
Yutaka Hasegawa

Publisher
Shingo Miyoshi

1998年1月22日初版第1刷発行
定価（本体 15,500円＋税）

発行所　ピエ・ブックス

〒170　東京都豊島区駒込4-14-6-301
編集　TEL:03-3949-5010 FAX:03-3949-5650
営業　TEL:03-3940-8302 FAX:03-3576-7361
e-mail: piebooks@bekkoame.or.jp

ISBN4-89444-054-7 C3070

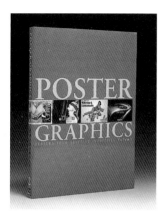

POSTER GRAPHICS Vol. 2
好評！業種別世界のポスター集大成、第2弾
Pages: 256 (192 in color) ¥16,505＋Tax
700 posters from the top creators in Japan and abroad are showcased in this book - classified by business. This invaluable reference makes it easy to compare design trends among various industries and corporations.

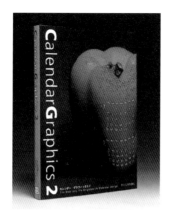

CALENDAR GRAPHICS Vol. 2
好評カレンダー・デザイン集の決定版、第2弾
Pages: 224 (192 in Color) ¥15,534＋Tax
The second volume of our popular 'Calendar Graphics' series features designs from about 250 1994 and 1995 calendars from around the world. A special collection that includes mass market as well as exclusive corporate PR calendars.

BROCHURE & PAMPHLET COLLECTION Vol. 4
好評！業種別カタログ・コレクション、第4弾
Pages: 224 (Full Color) ¥15,534＋Tax
The fourth volume in our popular "Brochure & Pamphlet" series. Twelve types of businesses are represented through artwork that really sells. This book conveys a sense of what's happening right now in the catalog design scene. A must for all creators.

BROCHURE DESIGN FORUM Vol. 3
世界の最新カタログ・コレクション、第3弾
Pages: 224 (Full Color) ¥15,534＋Tax
A special edition of our "Brochure & Pamphlet Collection" featuring 250 choice pieces that represent 70 types of businesses and are classified by business for handy reference. A compendium of the design scene at a glance.

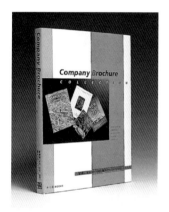

COMPANY BROCHURE COLLECTION
業種別（会社・学校・施設）案内グラフィックス
Pages: 224 (192 in Color) ¥15,534＋Tax
A special selection of brochures and catalogs ranging from admission manuals for colleges and universities, to amusement facility and hotel guidebooks, to corporate and organization profiles. The entries are classified by industry for easy reference.

COMPANY BROCHURE COLLECTION Vol. 2
業種別会社案内グラフィックス、第2弾！
Pages: 224 (Full Color) ¥15,534＋Tax
Showing imaginative layouts that present information clearly in a limited space, and design that effectively enhances corporate identity, this volume will prove to be an essential source book for graphic design work of the future.

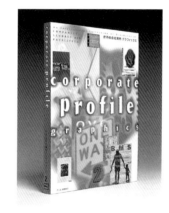

CORPORATE PROFILE GRAPHICS Vol. 2
世界の会社案内グラフィックス、第2弾
Pages: 224 (Full Color) ¥15,534＋Tax
An extensive collection of company brochures, annual reports, school facility guides and organization pamphlets. Brochures are fully detailed from cover to inner pages, illustrating clearly the importance of cohesiveness and flow. An essential catalog design reference volume.

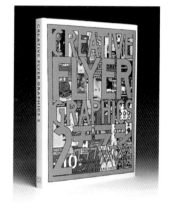

CREATIVE FLYER GRAPHICS Vol. 2
世界のフライヤーデザイン傑作集
Pages: 224 (Full Color) ¥15,534＋Tax
A pack of some 600 flyers and leaflets incorporating information from a variety of events including exhibitions, movies, plays, concerts, live entertainment and club events, as well as foods, cosmetics, electrical merchandise and travel packages.

EVENT FLYER GRAPHICS
世界のイベントフライヤー・コレクション
Pages: 224 (Full Color) ¥15,534＋Tax
Here's a special selection focusing on flyers promoting events. This upbeat selection covers a wide range of music events, as well as movies, exhibitions and the performing arts.

ADVERTISING FLYER GRAPHICS
衣・食・住・遊の商品チラシ特集
Pages: 224 (Full Color) ¥15,534＋Tax
The eye-catching flyers selected for this new collection represent a broad spectrum of businesses, and are presented in a loose classification covering four essential modern lifestyle themes: fashion, dining, home and leisure.

TRAVEL & LEISURE GRAPHICS
ホテル＆旅行案内グラフィックス
Pages: 224 (Full Color) ¥15,534＋Tax
A giant collection of some 400 pamphlets, posters and direct mailings exclusively created for hotels, inns, resort tours and amusement facilities.

SPECIAL EVENT GRAPHICS
世界のイベント・グラフィックス
Pages: 224 (192 in Color) ¥15,534＋Tax
A showcase for event graphics, introducing leaflets for exhibitions, fashion shows, all sorts of sales promotional campaigns, posters, premiums and actual installation scenes from events around the world. An invaluable and inspirational resource book, unique in the world of graphic publishing.

THE P·I·E COLLECTION

1, 2 & 3 COLOR GRAPHICS Vol. 2
1・2・3色グラフィックス、第2弾
Pages: 224 (Full Color) ¥15,534＋Tax
Even more ambitious in scale than the first volume, this second collection of graphics displays the unique talents of graphic designers who work with limited colors. An essential reference guide to effective, low-cost designing.

1 & 2 COLOR GRAPHICS
1色&2色デザインの大特集
Pages: 224 (Full Color) ¥15,534＋Tax
Powerful design achieved by restricting colors, unusual combinations of colors that grab the attention, enhanced stylishness of script... all artwork featured in this worldwide collection makes a dramatic visual impact. A useful book, too, for exploring the possibilities of low-cost design.

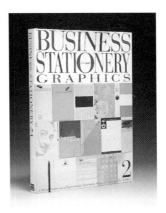

BUSINESS STATIONERY GRAPHICS Vol. 2
世界のレターヘッド・コレクション、第2弾
Pages: 224 (172 in Color) ¥15,534＋Tax
The second volume in our popular "Business Stationery Graphics" series. This publication focuses on letterheads, envelopes and business cards, all classified by business. This collection will serve artists and business people well.

NEW BUSINESS CARD GRAPHICS
最新版！ビジネスカード・グラフィックス
Pages: 224 (Full Color) ¥15,534＋Tax
A selection of 900 samples representing the works of top designers worldwide. Covering the broadest spectrum of business cards, it ranges from the trendiest to the most classy and includes highly original examples along the way.

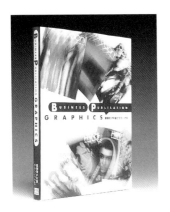

BUSINESS PUBLICATION GRAPHICS
業種別企業PR誌・フリーペーパーの集大成！
Pages: 224 (Full Color) ¥15,534＋Tax
This comprehensive graphic book introduces business publications created for a variety of business needs, including promotions from boutiques and department stores, exclusive clubs, local communities, and company newsletters.

BUSINESS PUBLICATION GRAPHICS Vol. 2
大好評！業種別PR誌の集大成、第2弾
Pages: 224 (Full Color) ¥15,534＋Tax
One volume offering more than 150 samples of regularly published PR and other informative magazines, covering different business sectors from fashion labels to non-profit organizations. This overviews the current trends in PR magazine design aimed at attracting the attention of a specific readership in commercial activities.

POSTCARD GRAPHICS Vol. 4
世界の業種別ポストカード・コレクション
Pages: 224 (192 in Color) ¥15,534＋Tax
Our popular "Postcard Graphics" series has been revamped for "Postcard Graphics Vol. 4." This first volume of the new version showcases approximately 1,000 pieces ranging from direct mailers to private greeting cards, selected from the best around the world.

SEASONAL CAMPAIGN GRAPHICS
デパート・ショップのキャンペーン広告特集
Pages: 224 (Full Color) ¥15,534＋Tax
A spirited collection of quality graphics for sales campaigns planned around the four seasons, Christmas, St. Valentine's Day and the Japanese gift-giving seasons, as well as for store openings, anniversaries, and similar events.

SHOPPING BAG GRAPHICS
世界の最新ショッピングバッグ・デザイン集
Pages: 224 (Full Color) ¥15,534＋Tax
Over 500 samples of the latest and best of the world's shopping bag designs from a wide range of retail businesses! This volume features a selection of shopping bags originating in Tokyo, NY, LA, London, Paris, Milan, and other major cities worldwide, presented here in a useful business classification.

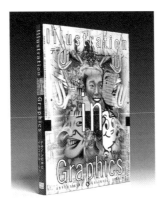

ILLUSTRATION IN GRAPHICS
イラストレーションを使った広告特集
Pages: 224 (Full Color) ¥15,534＋Tax
Delivering the message faster than photos and more accurately than words, illustration never fails to stir the imagination. This superb selection presents some 600 first-class illustrations for advertising from across the business spectrum and for editorial designs.

PRESENTATION GRAPHICS
制作の現場 プレゼンテーション・グラフィックス
Pages: 224 (Full Color) ¥15,500＋Tax
31 designers from 8 countries explain the production side of the creative process. Here are idea sketches, comps, presentations, and final works, all with explanatory notes by the designer. This is a unique volume that peeks behind the scenes of the creator's world.

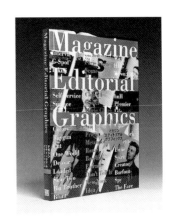

MAGAZINE EDITORIAL GRAPHICS
世界のエディトリアル＆カバーデザイン特集
Pages: 224 (Full Color) ¥15,500＋Tax
A special collection of editorial and cover designs. Stylish and sophisticated, 79 topical books from 9 countries were selected. Including top creators' graphic works, innovative fashion photography, and the latest typography, this is a true creator's bible for the New Age.

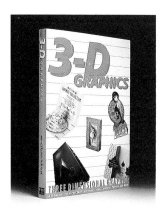

3-D GRAPHICS
3Dグラフィックスの大百科
Pages: 224 (192 in Color) ￥15,534＋Tax
350 works that demonstrate some of the finest examples of 3-D graphic methods, including DMs, catalogs, posters, POPs and more. The volume is a virtual encyclopedia of 3-D graphics.

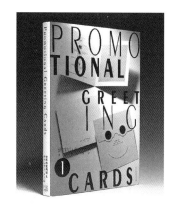

PROMOTIONAL GREETING CARDS
ADVERTISING GREETING CARDS Vol. 4
(English Title)
世界の案内状＆ダイレクトメール集大成
Pages: 224 (Full Color) ￥15,534＋Tax
A total of 500 examples of cards from designers around the world. A whole spectrum of stylish and inspirational cards, classified by function for easy reference.

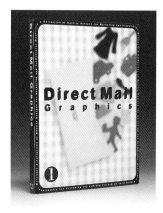

DIRECT MAIL GRAPHICS Vol. 1
衣・食・住のセールスＤＭ特集
Pages: 224 (Full Color) ￥15,534＋Tax
The long-awaited design collection featuring direct mailers that have outstanding sales impact and quality design. 350 of the best pieces, classified into 100 business categories. A veritable textbook of current direct marketing design.

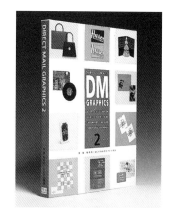

DIRECT MAIL GRAPHICS Vol. 2
好評！衣・食・住のセールスＤＭ特集！第２弾
Pages: 224 (Full Color) ￥15,534＋Tax
The second volume in our extremely popular "Direct Mail Graphics" series features a whole range of direct mailers for various purposes; from commercial announcements to seasonal greetings. Classfied by industry.

SUCCESSFUL DIRECT MAIL DESIGN
セールス効果の高いDMデザイン集！
Pages: 224 (Full Color) ￥15,500＋Tax
This collection features product flyers, service guides, shop opening and sale announcements, school and industrial promotions, and a variety of event invitations. A valuable book that captures the essence of today's direct marketing design.

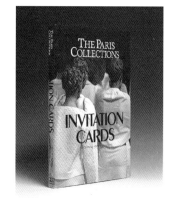

The Paris Collections / INVITATION CARDS
パリ・コレクションの招待状グラフィックス
Pages: 176 (Full Color) ￥13,396＋Tax
This book features 400 announcements for and invitations to the Paris Collections, produced by the world's top names in fashion over the past 10 years. A treasure trove of ideas and pure fun to browse through.

FASHION & COSMETICS GRAPHICS
ファッション＆コスメティック・グラフィックス
Pages: 208 (Full Color) ￥15,534＋Tax
A collection of promotional graphics from around the world produced for apparel, accessory and cosmetic brands at the avantgarde of the fashion industry. 40 brands featured in this book point the way toward future trends in advertising.

THE TOKYO TYPEDIRECTORS CLUB ANNUAL 1995-96
TDC 年鑑95-96
Pages: 250 (Full Color) ￥16,505＋Tax
A follow-up publication to Japan's only international graphic deisgn competition. Featuring 650 typographic artworks selected by THE TOKYO TYPEDIRECTORS CLUB, this book provides a window to the latest typographic design concepts worldwide.

The Production Index ARTIFILE Vol. 5
最新版プロダクション・クリエーター年鑑
Pages: 224 (Full Color) ￥12,136＋Tax
ARTIFILE 5 features artwork from a total of 100 top Japanese production companies and designers, along with company data and messages from the creators. An invaluable information source for anyone who needs to keep up with the latest developments in the graphic scene.

CARTOON CHARACTER COLLECTION
5500種のキャラクターデザイン大百科
Pages: 480 (B&W) ￥3,600＋Tax
A collection of illustrations from successful character artists. People, animals, plants, food, vehicles, landscapes, sports, seasons... Nearly 5,500 works are presented, conveniently categorized. A collection full of ideas sure to come in handy when designing greeting cards and illustrations.

CATALOGUE AND PAMPHLET COLLECTION
/ Soft Jacket
業種別商品カタログ特集／ソフトカバー
Pages: 224 (Full Color) ￥3,689＋Tax
A collection of the world's most outstanding brochures, catalogs and leaflets classified by industry such as fashion, restaurants, music, interiors and sporting goods. Presenting each piece in detail from cover to inside pages. This title is an indispensable sourcebook for all graphic designers and CI professionals.

SPORTS GRAPHICS / Soft Jacket
世界のスポーツグッズ・コレクション
／ソフトカバー
Pages: 224 (192 in Color) ￥3,689＋Tax
A Collection of 1,000 bold sporting goods graphic works from all over the world. A wide variety of goods are shown, including uniforms, bags, shoes and other gear. Covers all sorts of sports: basketball, skiing, surfing, and many, many more.

THE P·I·E COLLECTION

**LABELS AND TAGS COLLECTION Vol. 1
/ Soft Jacket**
ラベル＆タグ・コレクション／ソフトカバー
Pages: 224 (192 in Color) ￥3,689＋Tax
Nowhere is brand recognition more important
than in Japan. Here is a collection of 1,600
labels and tags from Japan's 450 top fashion
names with page after page of women's and
men's clothing and sportswear designs.

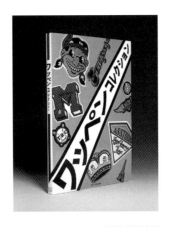

**FASHION INSIGNIA COLLECTION
/ Soft Jacket**
ワッペン・コレクション／ソフトカバー
Pages: 224 (Full Color) ￥3,689＋Tax
Over 300 designs were scrutinized for this
collection of 1000 outstanding emblems and
embroidered motifs. Visually exciting, they
make innovative use of materials and
compliment the fashions with which they are
worn.

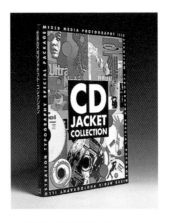

CD JACKET COLLECTION / Soft Jacket
世界のCDジャケット・コレクション
／ソフトカバー
Pages: 224 (192 in Color) ￥3,689＋Tax
Featuring 700 of the world's most imaginative
CD and LP covers from all musical genres,
this is a must-have book for all design and
music professionals.

POSTCARD COLLECTION Vol. 2 / Soft Jacket
好評 ポストカード・コレクション、第2弾
／ソフトカバー
Pages: 230 (Full Color) ￥3,689＋Tax
Welcome to the colorful world of postcards,
with 1200 postcards created by artists from
all over the world classified according to the
business of the client.

POSTCARD COLLECTION / Soft Jacket
世界のポストカード・コレクション
／ソフトカバー
Pages: 240 (Full Color) ￥3,689＋Tax
Postcards from top Japanese designers,
fashion brands, and famous shops. This
book shows how designers, using beautiful
photos and fun illustrations, pack a lot of
creativity into a postcard's limited space.

DIAGRAM COLLECTION
世界のダイアグラム・デザイン集大成
Pages: 224 (192 in Color) ￥3,700＋Tax
Graphs, charts, maps, architectural diagrams
and plans, product and scientific illustrations.
Almost 400 diagrams selected from designs
sent to us by some of the world's most
talented creators. This invaluable volume
shows the many possibilities of diagram
design.

WORLD BUSINESS CARD COLLECTION
世界の名刺コレクション Vol. 2
Pages: 224 (192 in Color) ￥3,700＋Tax
From personal and business cards, bursting
with individuality, to colorfully creative shop
cards, we introduce nearly 1,000 of the best.
Limited in size, these designs mix fun and
cleverness, and will impress and delight you
with their originality.

カタログ・新刊のご案内について
総合カタログ、新刊案内をご希望の方は、はさみ込みのアンケートはがきを
ご返送いただくか、90円切手同封の上、ピエ・ブックス宛お申し込み下さい。

CATALOGUES ET INFORMATIONS SUR LES NOUVELLES PUBLICATIONS
Si vous désirez recevoir un exemplaire gratuit de notre catalogue général
ou des détails sur nos nouvelles publications, veuillez compléter la carte
réponse incluse et nous la retourner par courrierou par fax.

CATALOGS and INFORMATION ON NEW PUBLICATIONS
If you would like to receive a free copy of our general catalog or
details of our new publications, please fill out the enclosed postcard
and return it to us by mail or fax.

CATALOGE und INFORMATIONEN ÜBER NEUE TITLE
Wenn Sie unseren Gesamtkatalog oder Detailinformationen über
unsere neuen Titel wünschen, fullen Sie bitte die beigefügte Postkarte
aus und schicken Sie sie uns per Post oder Fax.

ピエ・ブックス
〒170 東京都豊島区駒込 4-14-6-301
TEL: 03-3940-8302 FAX: 03-3576-7361

P·I·E BOOKS
#301, 4-14-6, Komagome, Toshima-ku, Tokyo 170 JAPAN
TEL: 03-3940-8302 FAX: 03-3576-7361